The Lovers' Book

The Lovers' Book

KATE GRIBBLE

St. Martin's Press ❧ New York

www.stmartins.com

Illustration on pages 47–49 © 2008 by David Woodroffe

Library of Congress Cataloging-in-Publication Data

Gribble, Kate.
   The lovers' book / Kate Gribble. — 1st U.S. ed.
     p. cm.
   ISBN-13: 978-0-312-53294-9
   ISBN-10: 0-312-53294-6
   1. Man-woman relationships.   2. Dating (Social customs)   3. Sexual attraction.   4. Love.   I. Title.
   HQ801.G73 2009
   306.73'4—dc22   2008040012

First published in Great Britain by Michael O'Mara Books Limited

First U.S. Edition: February 2009

10 9 8 7 6 5 4 3 2 1

To Duncan,
my inspiration and my soulmate

Contents

♥ ♥

# *Introduction*

L OVE. It's a many-splendored thing. It makes the world go round. Love is patient, love is kind. Love sees no faults (perhaps because love is blind). Love conquers all. All you need is love . . .

Clearly, love has got quite a reputation for itself, but it more than lives up to it. Whether you've been with your lover for decades or just days, you'll be all too familiar with that heart-racing feeling of happiness you get whenever you're in their company. Nothing compares to them, nothing compares to your love for them, and nothing is more important than expressing your love for them.

The lover who's best at everything knows that the best way to charm their other half is with thoughtful gestures tailored to their soulmate's idiosyncrasies. After all, you're the person who knows your lover best. No one else in the world can make them happier.

Every now and then, though, even the best lovers need a little inspiration for romantic deeds. *The Lovers' Book* is a treasure trove of idyllic ideas and soulful suggestions that will make your partner fall head over heels in love with you – again, and again, and again . . .

Learn how to make a homemade Valentine's card, to personalize an advent calendar (for the run-up to your anniversary), to prepare the perfect breakfast in bed, and to write a love poem. Get inspiration for mini-breaks and day trips, as well as everyday gestures that will knock your sweetheart's socks off.

The book also takes a look at the most famous lovers of all time, reviews the tradition of courtly love, investigates the

♥ ♥

history of Valentine's Day and records real-life instances of remarkable romance. All in all, it's a delightful celebration of the joys of being in love.

Always remember that no matter what you do, to your other half you'll always be *the lover who's best at everything.*

'There is only one happiness in life – to love and be loved.'

GEORGE SAND

In the Beginning There Was Love

EXCHANGING stories about falling in love is a little like that Cadbury's Crème Egg slogan. How did you meet yours? Everybody has their own story to tell. Here's a collection of unusual routes to romantic bliss taken by real-life lovers.

Against the Odds

It's a truth universally acknowledged that you can't help who you fall in love with. And, sometimes, love isn't easy. Yet as the proverb goes, love will always out. That was certainly true in the case of June and Heinz Fellbrich. When they got hitched in 1947, their wedding photographs made headlines around the world – for June was a young British girl, and Heinz a German POW (prisoner of war).

On their wedding night, Heinz had to leave the celebrations early to be locked up back inside the POW camp. The newlyweds were regularly spat at in the street and received sackloads

♥♥

of hate mail. But they recently celebrated their sixtieth wedding anniversary.

June said she didn't regret a thing: 'I know it was worth it because I loved him and still do, and that's the secret of our married life – love.'

> 'The thing about falling in love, is that if you do it right, you never have to hit the ground.'
>
> **KENDALL LEPITZKI**

Written in the ~~Stars~~ Brochure

Kieron and Amanda Dudley met each other through work. Not so unusual, true. However, while in the line of duty at the Dunston Hall hotel, the pair, though just colleagues, ended up posing as newlyweds for the hotel's wedding brochure in September 2004. Almost three years later, they ended up holding their very own wedding reception there – this time for real!

We Just Double-Clicked

Many couples these days first meet on the Internet, via chat rooms or on dating websites. One pair found each other through online marketplace eBay, after singer James Blunt put his sister Emily 'up for sale'.

'Damsel in distress seeks knight in shining armor. Desperate to get to a funeral in southern Ireland, please help,' the ad read. Big brother James was determined to help out his sibling, who was distraught at the thought of missing an important memorial service because of transport disasters.

♥♥

The highest bidder happened to be millionaire Guy Harrison, who flew Emily to the funeral in his helicopter (as you do). The besotted couple married in Hampshire in 2007.

TIP!

Every now and again, make a point of rereading the e-mails and love letters you wrote your lover (and received from them) in the early days of your relationship. The feelings of excitement, anticipation and overpowering emotion will come flooding back in an instant.

Love at First Sight

It's the great myth in romance . . . or is it totally true? England footballer David Beckham certainly thinks so. He fell for his future wife, Victoria Adams, before the pair had even met.

In November 1996, he saw the video for the Spice Girls' single 'Say You'll Be There', and was instantly smitten with 'Posh'. He remembers: 'I pointed at the screen and told Gary [Neville], "That's the girl for me and I am going to get her." It was her eyes, her face. She's my idea of perfection. I was sure just from seeing her on that video that she was the one I wanted, and I knew that if she wanted me we would be together forever.'

And they both lived happily ever after . . .

'We love because it's the only true adventure.'
NIKKI GIOVANNI

The Science of Love

A RACING heart, flushed cheeks, breathlessness, a shortened attention span, a debilitating fever: oh, the symptoms of love are far-reaching, and you're too far gone to care. But what's the science behind the physical effects of falling in love?

A Step-By-Step Scientific Guide to Falling in Love

Helen Fisher of Rutgers University in New Jersey is one of the best-known researchers in the field of love's biochemistry. She has discovered that there are three key stages when it comes to falling in love, each of which is governed by a different set of chemicals. Here's a simple summary of her research, offering an insight into how some of those chemicals make us feel.

Step One: Lust

Fisher says this stage will 'get you out looking for anything'. Not the most romantic period, then. This stage is fuelled by the sex hormones estrogen and testosterone.

♥♥♥

Step Two: Attraction

This is when that crazy neurotransmitter serotonin starts whizzing in our brains; it's joined by dopamine and adrenalin, the latter of which accounts for the racing heart and sweaty palms that all lovers experience.

During this phase, a loss of appetite may occur, and you'll probably need less sleep than usual because of the buzz you're getting from the feeling of attraction.

Step Three: Attachment

Not all love affairs progress to this stage, but if you're meant to be, you'll definitely be affected by the hormones oxytocin and the less-than-sexy-sounding vasopressin. Oxytocin is a hormone that increases trust and encourages bonding. It's released during orgasm, so the more often a couple makes love, the more likely they are to become inseparable.

Falling for Pheromones

Pheromones are invisible chemical substances unwittingly released by humans, as well as other mammals, which signal many things, including sexual desire and basic genetic blueprints. Health educator Deb Levine once dubbed the human pheromone 'the sexual scent of attraction'.

Indeed, it's now thought that pheromones play a major role when two people fall for each other. A 1999 article in *Psychology Today* revealed that the way others perceive our unique scent is a highly selective process, wired by genetics.

Rather unromantically, we usually smell best to a person whose immunity to disease differs most from our own. The theory goes that combining the two in-built genetic defences

♥♥♥

through reproduction will result in stronger, healthier children: the instinctive aim behind all sexual attraction.

So, the next time you inhale your lover's particular scent (which may well be your favorite smell in the whole world), remember that what you're reveling in is not only their olfactory trace, but also their pheromones . . . pheromones which confirm, through your mutual attraction, that you and your partner are truly meant to be.

SCIENTIFIC STUDIES

In 2002, Australian researchers disproved a 1970s theory that marriage drove women up the wall, instead finding that both sexes are happier when married. From a survey of 10,641 Australian adults, married women with children were the least likely to suffer mental health problems, while 25 percent of men and women were depressed when single.

In 2005, American scientists concluded that opposites did not attract, when their study of married couples found that the happiest marriages were those in which the partners were similarly matched in terms of personality and beliefs.

Lovers in History

THE heat of some lovers' passion is so fiery that it leaves its mark not only on them, but also on the rest of the world. The following couples have gone down in history as the most desperately-in-love duos of all time.

Mark Antony and Cleopatra

In the first century B.C., Cleopatra was Queen of Egypt, while Roman soldier Mark Antony was leading the emerging Roman Empire as part of the Second Triumvirate with Lepidus and Octavian.

They had first met in 46 B.C. when Julius Caesar first brought Cleopatra to Rome, and fate was to throw them together four years later when Antony visited Egypt to investigate Cleopatra on behalf of Rome. Instead he fell madly in love with her (even though he was already married). The lovers soon established a court of pleasure, luxury and indulgence in Alexandria, much to Rome's concern and disapproval, and are said to have married in 36 B.C.

Meanwhile, Lepidus had retired from power, leaving Antony and Octavian to lead the Empire. Though Antony came back to Rome briefly and spearheaded more fighting for the Empire's cause, he could not bear to be apart from Cleopatra, and soon returned to Egypt to be by her side, caring not a whit for Rome's increasing anger at his actions. In 32 B.C., the Roman Senate stripped Antony of his powers, and Octavian set out to destroy the two lovers.

The rival fleets engaged in battle off the coast of Actium in 31 B.C., but Antony was outwitted by Octavian, and forced to return hastily to Alexandria. Back in Egypt, the couple tried to defend themselves against the inexorable approaching force of the Empire's army, but were fighting a losing battle.

The captivating story of the Egyptian Queen and her Roman warrior lover inspired both Shakespeare's 1606 play *Antony and Cleopatra* and MGM's blockbusting 1963 movie *Cleopatra*, which starred Elizabeth Taylor and Richard Burton as the paramours.

It is said that when Antony heard false rumours of Cleopatra's death, he committed suicide by falling on his sword. Thus, with her beloved Antony gone and the heartless Octavian now in power in Egypt, Cleopatra, too, decided to take her own life. Famously, she allowed a poisonous asp to bite her, thus bringing an end to one of the world's most memorable love affairs.

ANTONY: I am dying, Egypt, dying; only
I here importune death awhile, until
Of many thousand kisses the poor last
I lay upon thy lips.
[. . .]

▼▼

CLEOPATRA: And welcome, welcome! Die where thou hast
lived:
Quicken with kissing: had my lips that power,
Thus would I wear them out.

Antony and Cleopatra, Act IV, Scene xv,
WILLIAM SHAKESPEARE

Shah Jahan and Mumtaz Mahal

This real-life romance provided the foundations of the world's
most recognizable monument to love: the Taj Mahal in India.

In 1612, the emperor of the Mughal Empire, Shah Jahan,
married the young Arjumand Banu Begum, a Persian princess,
who was renamed Mumtaz Mahal after the wedding. Mumtaz
was undoubtedly the emperor's favorite wife and the pair were
impossibly in love throughout their marriage.

In 1631, tragedy struck, when Mumtaz died while giving birth
to their fourteenth child. Devastated, Shah Jahan determined
to erect a beautiful building in memory of his wife. Work
immediately began on the soon-to-be-celebrated Taj Mahal.

It took over twenty years to complete – and the sweat and
toil of 22,000 workers and 1,000 elephants – but it was worth it.
When the building was finished, it rose magnificently from its
spot beside the Jamuna River, semi-precious stones laid into its
exterior walls, a marble minaret in each corner, a towering
dome, and gardens designed in a vision of Paradise. To this day,
it is considered one of the finest examples of Indian Islamic
architecture.

When Shah Jahan died in 1666, he was laid to rest beside his
wife, in an underground crypt built beneath his enduring
monument to her memory.

▼▼

♥♥

Queen Victoria and Prince Albert

Queen Victoria ascended the English throne in 1837, at the age of eighteen. Three years later, she married her first cousin, Prince Albert of Saxe-Coburg-Gotha. The couple were deeply in love and remained so for the rest of their marriage, during which time they had nine children.

Albert became a valued adviser to his wife, particularly in the areas of diplomacy and politics, but in December 1861, at the age of forty-two, he died suddenly of typhoid fever.

Her beloved husband's death came as a terrible shock to Queen Victoria. She immediately withdrew from public life and sank into a depression. It was three years before she next appeared in public and five before she could be persuaded to open Parliament. For the rest of her sixty-three-year reign, she continued to mourn Albert and dressed only in black.

> 'My life as a happy one is ended! The world is gone for me! If I must live on . . . it is henceforth for our poor fatherless children – for my unhappy country, which has lost all in losing him – and in only doing what I know and feel he would wish.'
>
> **QUEEN VICTORIA** in a letter dated December 20, 1861, to Leopold I, King of the Belgians

Like Shah Jahan, Victoria wanted to build a monument in memory of her husband, and so she commissioned the famous architect Sir Gilbert Scott to create the Albert Memorial – officially titled the 'Prince Consort National Memorial'. Unveiled in 1876, and situated in Kensington Gardens in London, it is one of the most impressive high-Victorian gothic spectacles in existence, employing a Parnassus frieze, marble figures and gilded bronze statues to breathtaking effect.

♥♥

♥♥♥

On January 22, 1901, almost forty years after Albert's death, Queen Victoria followed her beloved to the grave and was laid to rest beside him at the Frogmore Royal Mausoleum at Windsor. Inscribed above the mausoleum door are Victoria's words: 'Farewell best beloved, here at last I shall rest with thee, with thee in Christ I shall rise again.'

Annie Oakley and Frank Butler

Annie Oakley was born Phoebe Ann Mosey in Ohio in August 1860. She was a self-trained markswoman who, by the age of fifteen, had made enough money from the sale of game she shot that she was able to pay off her mother's mortgage.

In 1881, cocky Frank E. Butler came to her state, boasting that he could beat any local marksman who dared take him on. As one half of a famous shooting act, Baughman and Butler, he had no doubts he would come out on top, but he had reckoned without young Phoebe Ann. She won their contest hands down – and Butler was smitten. Married the following year, Frank eventually gave up his own illustrious career in favor of promoting that of his wife, who took the stage name Annie Oakley (though she was always Mrs. Frank Butler in her personal life) and the world by storm as a star in Buffalo Bill's Wild West show.

They were happily married for forty-four years until Annie's death in 1926. Frank, grief-stricken, survived for only another eighteen days before he too passed away.

The gun-toting pair were the inspiration behind the popular 1946 Irving Berlin musical *Annie, Get Your Gun*.

♥♥♥

Grace Kelly and Prince Rainier of Monaco

Grace Kelly's love affair had a fairy-tale quality to it, as the movie star who became a real princess. Born in November 1929, the actress landed her first role in the 1951 film *Fourteen Hours.* A year later, her appearance as Amy Kane in the popular *High Noon* set her career alight; later movies included Alfred Hitchcock's *Dial M for Murder* (1954), *Rear Window* (1954) and *To Catch a Thief* (1955).

Her role in the 1954 film *The Country Girl* won her the Academy Award for Best Actress, and it was while promoting this movie at the Cannes Film Festival in May 1955, that she encountered Prince Rainier, the handsome heir to the kingdom of Monaco. After a whirlwind romance, the two became engaged the following January and later married on April 19, 1956. Grace gave up her film career in favor of becoming Her Serene Highness Princess Grace of Monaco. The couple had three children, Caroline, Albert and Stephanie.

In September 1982, Princess Grace died tragically in a car accident in Monaco. After her death, Prince Rainier opened a public rose garden in her memory: roses were his wife's favorite flowers.

Ronald and Nancy Reagan

The fortieth president and his wife enjoyed a happy fifty-two-year marriage. Indeed the actor Charlton Heston once commented that theirs was 'the greatest love affair in the history of the American presidency'.

Former Hollywood star Ronald met Nancy in the early 1950s while president of the Screen Actors Guild. At their first

♥♥♥

meeting he'd intended to leave early, owing to a busy schedule the next day, but they were still excitedly chatting at 3 a.m. Nancy once said of their courtship: 'I don't know if it was exactly love at first sight, but it was pretty close.'

The future president proposed in their favorite restaurant, Chasen's:

'Let's get married,' he fired off.

'Let's,' Nancy shot back.

The couple wed in March 1952, in Los Angeles, and later had two children, Patricia and Ronald.

In 1980, during Ronald Senior's grueling presidential campaign, their passion didn't flag for one moment, and they would always kiss as though it was for the last time. An NBC White House correspondent remarked of their embraces: 'We [journalists] would turn aside because we felt that there was something very special, private and wonderful going on between them.'

During Reagan's tenure as President (1981–9), the couple used to hide love notes for each other all over the White House, and walk hand in hand around the grounds.

In 1994, he announced he was suffering from Alzheimer's disease – and his primary concern, as it had always been, was for his wife. 'I only wish there was some way I could spare Nancy from this painful experience,' he said.

Reagan passed away in 2004, aged ninety-three, after Nancy had carefully and lovingly managed what she termed his 'long goodbye'.

'Our relationship is very special. We were very much in love and still are. When I say my life began with Ronnie, well, it's true. It did. I can't imagine life without him.'

NANCY REAGAN, *Vanity Fair* (1988)

♥♥♥

CASANOVA

No rundown of lovers in history would be complete without a word on Casanova, the most famous of all time, whose name has become synonymous with the art of love.

Giacomo Casanova was born in Venice in April 1725. A sickly child, he grew up to be an explorer and writer, but his most famous adventures involved his seduction of women, which he described in his notorious memoirs *Histoire de Ma Vie* (Story of My Life). He is reputed to have made love up to six times a night, and bedded countless women, including a nun. But far from being a heartless Lothario, by all accounts Casanova cared deeply for his many lovers, respecting their intelligence as well as their physical beauty. He wrote modestly: 'I was born for the opposite sex.'

Many myths abound about Casanova, including how he would eat fifty oysters (an infamous aphrodisiac) for breakfast every day. His legend has captivated filmmakers and television producers across the world, and resulted in numerous adaptations of his fascinating life story.

'I will never admit that it [love] is a trifle or a vanity. It is a kind of madness over which philosophy has no power at all.'

GIACOMO CASANOVA

The Couple That Plays Together

EVER heard the maxim 'the couple that plays together stays together'? Though it might sometimes seem difficult to find moments in which to share quality time with your lover – what with work, friends, kids and a host of other commitments all making demands on your schedule – always try to make the time. Remember, a relationship isn't just wonderful because of the romance: fun has a lot to do with it, too!

Set aside special moments just for the two of you. Whether it's a day out, an evening or a weekend away, make proper use of the time you have dedicated to one another, and remind each other just why you fell in love in the first place.

'We tend to our marriage. You have to spend time away from the kids and stay up late and talk, go to the movies or do the crossword puzzle together. My husband and I still have date nights, and I look forward to them all week.'

MICHELLE PFEIFFER,
married to TV producer David E. Kelley

You and your lover probably share a number of interests; they might even have been the reason you first met. Keep those shared passions burning – act in plays together; go to football

♥♥

games; travel the world; sample new cuisines in all the restaurants your town has to offer.

Of course, there's nothing to stop you broadening your interests, too. In fact, embarking on new hobbies together is not only fun – you may also make fresh discoveries about your partner . . . just when you thought you had them sussed.

Here are some suggestions of couple-tastic activities, whether you want to kick-start new pastimes or simply enjoy a great night out.

Top Date Ideas

Take a Hike

Be it a romantic stroll or a ten-mile ramble, relish the two of you being at one with nature. For example, one couple opted for an extreme type of hiking togetherness when they embarked on a 2007 quest to tackle Scotland's 284 Munros (mountains over 3,000 feet high) completely in the nude. At the time of writing, they'd completed fifteen of them.

Jazz it Up

Pop along to your local live jazz club and take in the chilled vibe over dinner.

Step Back in Time

Relive your dissolute adolescences at a school-disco-themed party, or turn on the vintage charm by attending a 1940s-style tea dance: both in full costume.

♥♥

Dance the Night Away

Ballroom, jive, salsa or the ubiquitous freestyle – whatever rocks your world. Best of all, you'll be in your lover's arms all evening.

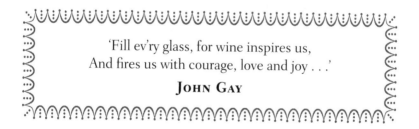

TIP!
Take a course of lessons to learn a new dance style,
to up the ante on the fancy footwork.

Neck the Nectar

Enjoy a wine-tasting session together at a vineyard or winery.

'Fill ev'ry glass, for wine inspires us,
And fires us with courage, love and joy . . .'
JOHN GAY

Stargaze Till the Sun Comes Up

Even if your local area doesn't have an observatory with public access, spend an evening taking in the night sky (with or without a telescope). Cuddle up close, crane your heads back and wish upon any falling stars you might glimpse in the heavens.

If you're city mice, it makes sense to get as far away from those bright lights as you can and find a quiet spot in the countryside.

♥ ♥ ♥

Paint the Town Red

Immerse yourselves in art: visit galleries, buy paintings and practice your own artful techniques. Eventually, why not try painting each other?

In August 2007, George Aye proposed to his girlfriend Sara Cantor in a Chicago art gallery. But it wasn't just any old exhibition he'd taken her to – George had staged the whole evening, right down to the extras he'd hired to play the roles of other gallery enthusiasts.

The centerpiece of his master plan was a piece of art that he had created from foam which, when viewed from a specific angle, spelled out: 'Will you marry me?'

When Sara spotted the message, she also discovered George down on one knee. Bowled over, she accepted his proposal in an 'artbeat.

Get Fit

These days, everyone knows that doing a spell of exercise can release feel-good chemicals called endorphins. As love can do much the same thing, who knows how good you'll feel after a workout session with your partner?

♥♥♥♥♥♥♥♥♥♥♥♥♥♥♥♥♥♥♥♥♥♥♥♥♥♥♥♥♥♥♥♥♥♥♥♥♥♥♥

♥♥♥♥♥♥♥♥♥♥♥♥♥♥♥♥♥♥♥♥♥♥♥♥♥♥♥♥♥♥♥♥♥♥♥♥♥

Throw a Party

There's nothing like the pressure of hosting a do to bring the two of you closer together. Have fun planning the menu and the theme – you could even make it a fancy-dress party to add to the occasion.

Top Ten Double-Act Fancy-Dress Costumes

1 Batman and Catwoman

2 Bonnie and Clyde

3 Miss Piggy and Kermit the Frog

4 Antony and Cleopatra

5 Little Red Riding Hood and the Big Bad Wolf

6 Cinderella and Prince Charming

7 Danny and Sandy from *Grease*

8 Queen Elizabeth II and Prince Philip

9 Superman and Lois Lane

10 Ozzy and Sharon Osbourne

Hitting the Shops

Shopping can sometimes cause all manner of rows, but you can make your outing extra special by avoiding the high street and losing yourselves in secondhand bookstores, quirky gift boutiques and eccentric antiques shops.

♥♥♥♥♥♥♥♥♥♥♥♥♥♥♥♥♥♥♥♥♥♥♥♥♥♥♥♥♥♥♥♥♥♥♥♥♥

♥♥♥♥♥♥♥♥♥♥♥♥♥♥♥♥♥♥♥♥♥♥♥♥♥♥♥♥♥♥♥♥♥♥♥♥♥♥

Float Your Boat

Take to the high seas (or a canal) in a hired boat. Be it a yacht, punt, rowboat or canoe, find your sea legs with your sweetheart.

♥ ♥ ♥

Go the Extra Mile

Be extravagant and travel somewhere far away just for a single evening's date. Okay, so it won't look great for your carbon footprint, but an impetuous decision to head for the hills (for dinner at that discreet little place you know) simply smacks of spontaneous romance.

> 'Anyone can be passionate,
> but it takes real lovers to be silly.'
> **ROSE FRANKEN**

Home Alone

While partying and going out on the town have their place, sometimes there's nothing nicer than spending time at home together. Here are some ideas to make the most of your time in your little love nest.

An Intimate Candlelit Supper

Cooking for your partner at home is one of the most romantic ways to spend an evening – you could even try some of the recipes suggested in this book. Alternatively, your lover's favorite dish will always go down well.

♥♥♥♥♥♥♥♥♥♥♥♥♥♥♥♥♥♥♥♥♥♥♥♥♥♥♥♥♥♥♥♥♥♥♥♥♥♥

♥♥♥♥♥♥♥♥♥♥♥♥♥♥♥♥♥♥♥♥♥♥♥♥♥♥♥♥♥♥♥♥♥♥♥♥♥♥

To make the evening extra special, you can really go to town. Why not make an ice sculpture as a table centerpiece? It's not as hard as it sounds: you can buy ready-made moulds in the shape of a swan as well as many other 3-D forms.

One important note: don't forget the candles, but keep them away from the ice!

♥ ♥ ♥

Play Your Cards Right

Crank up the competitive edge with a night of game playing. Who will fold first? Paul McGee, relationships expert and author of *S.U.M.O. Your Relationships*, says: 'Healthy competition can bring energy to a relationship.'

That's 'healthy competition', remember, not 'determined to win at all costs'!

Tip!

If you're playing poker, add a fun factor by creating 'poker names' for each other that you have to use all night, with penalties (of your own choosing) if one of you forgets. Take a U.S. state and add another word to generate your tag – for example, you could call yourselves 'Texas Beige' or 'Dakota Daiquiri'.

Do it Yourselves

Home decorating sometimes gets a bad press for being boring, but planning, painting and creating a new look for your snug

♥♥♥♥♥♥♥♥♥♥♥♥♥♥♥♥♥♥♥♥♥♥♥♥♥♥♥♥♥♥♥♥♥♥♥♥♥♥

burrow is fantastic fun, and you'll get to enjoy the results for years to come.

Movie Magic

Spend an evening in cinematic heaven, right on your very own sofa. Dim the lights, heat the buttered popcorn and play a DVD.

See page 74 for a list of the top-ten most romantic films, or you could always opt for a horror movie (the scary bits provide a great excuse to leap into each other's arms).

Photo Fun

While away an afternoon filling photo albums or picture frames with your favorite snaps. You could also take advantage of the time to stage an impromptu photo shoot, by dressing yourselves up to the nines and posing for each other. Say cheese!

The Weekend Papers

The idyll that is stretching out and reading the weekend papers together has long been appreciated as a perfect pastime for lovers. Gently squabble over who gets which sections first, and read aloud the bits that make you laugh, cry or just plain confused.

Get an Early Night

No further explanation necessary.

▼▼▼▼▼▼▼▼▼▼▼▼▼▼▼▼▼▼▼▼▼▼▼▼▼▼▼▼▼▼▼▼▼

Television Heaven

We all have our favorite TV shows that we follow religiously and can discuss for hours on end, so why not include your partner in your passion? A night on the sofa sharing their enthusiasm, snuggled up tight as the theme song plays, can be one of the best ways to spend an evening together.

It Takes Two

As a couple, you're a special, intimate unit. Consequently there are some things only two can do . . .

1. Ride a tandem

2. Run a three-legged race

3. Camp in a two-man tent

4. Arm wrestle

5. Tango

6. Sing a duet

7. Take advantage of 2-for-1 ticket offers

8. Go for a drive in a two-seater convertible

9. Dine at a table for two

10. Make love

> 'It takes two to lie, Marge. One to lie and one to listen.'
> **HOMER SIMPSON**, *The Simpsons*

▼▼▼▼▼▼▼▼▼▼▼▼▼▼▼▼▼▼▼▼▼▼▼▼▼▼▼▼▼▼▼▼▼

Love Facts and Figures

SURELY the only sum you need to know when you're in love is $1 + 1 = 2$? Of course, but these love-based facts and figures may add to your amusement . . .

Eminent anthropologist George Peter Murdock claimed in his *Ethnographic Atlas* that of 849 societies, 70 percent are polygynous. In other words, polygamy (one husband with two or more wives) is the most common form of marriage in the world.

According to the Office for National Statistics, the number of couples getting married in the UK each year is falling. In 2004, there were 313,550 weddings, but that figure fell by almost 10 percent the following year to only 283,730.

Denmark was the first country to give same-sex couples equal rights with married heterosexuals, when legislation was passed in 1989. Twelve years later, the Netherlands became the first country to grant full civil marriage rights to gay couples.

▼ ▼

The world's longest engagement lasted sixty-seven years. Octavio Guillen proposed to fifteen-year-old Adriana Martinez in Mexico in 1902, but it wasn't until June 1969 that they finally got round to exchanging their vows. They were both eighty-two on their wedding day.

Where you live may also determine how successful you will be in achieving a long-lasting marriage. You can increase your chances of wedded bliss simply by living in the right place. Some of the best cities for couples, according to *Forbes,* are:

1. Denver, Colorado

2. San Antonio, Texas

3. Phoenix, Arizona

4. Atlanta, Georgia

5. San Francisco, California

In Denver, only 20 percent of couples separated or divorced – the national average is 43 percent.

British couple Thomas and Elizabeth Morgan are the oldest married couple in history as far as their aggregate age is concerned. They married on May 4, 1809, and remained together for eighty-one years and 260 days, until Elizabeth's death on January 19, 1891. When she died, Elizabeth was 105 years and

▼ ▼

two days old, and Thomas was 104 years and 260 days old – an aggregate age of 209 years, 262 days. Phew!

'The love we give away is the only love we keep.'
ELBERT HUBBARD

The longest marriage in the world lasted an impressive eighty-six years. Taiwanese couple Liu Yung-yang and Yang Wan wed in April 1917, when Liu Yung-yang was twenty-one and his young bride was seventeen. They both lived into their early hundreds and their children, grandchildren and great-grandchildren totalled a stunning 110.

Although they had got married at a conventional age, they had known each other since childhood: in accordance with an ancient Taiwanese tradition, Yang Wan was sent to live with her future spouse's family at the age of five. The long marriage ended in 2003 when 103-year-old Yang Wan died of natural causes.

'Love is the perfect sum / Of all delight.'
TOBIAS HUME

Will You Be My Valentine?

EVERY year on February 14, we celebrate Valentine's Day, an occasion when lovers around the world take the opportunity to honor (or declare) their passion for their partner, through traditions such as sending cards with romantic messages or giving flowers. It is named after the patron saint of lovers, St. Valentine.

It's a Date

Mid-February has always been a key period in calendars of celebrations. The ancient Athenians are said to have held month-long festivities between mid-January and mid-February in honor of the marriage of the gods Zeus and Hera, while in Ancient Rome the fertility festival Lupercalia fell at this time. In the year 496, Pope Gelasius I announced that the feast of St. Valentine would be on February 14.

Who Was St. Valentine?

The identity of the patron saint of lovers is shrouded in mystery. For a start, dozens of early Christian martyrs were called St. Valentine – in fact, until 1969, the Catholic Church formally recognized a total of eleven Valentine's Days.

However, only two of these saints were commemorated on February 14: Valentine of Rome and Valentine of Terni. Confusingly, neither was known to be particularly associated with love.

♥♥♥

A further theory contends that St. Valentine was a priest in third-century Rome. When Emperor Claudius II declared that young men were forbidden to marry (a consequence of his observation that single men made better soldiers), Valentine is said to have flouted the law and covertly conducted marriages. In time, his disobedience was discovered and he was subsequently executed – supposedly the night before February 14.

One final legend reveals that Valentine was once imprisoned. While in jail, he fell in love with a girl who visited him there, and from then on he would write her love notes from his cell, signed 'from your Valentine'.

Say it With Words

The medieval poet Geoffrey Chaucer provided one of the first written references to Valentine's Day and its celebration of love and partnership. In his poem *The Parliament of Fowls*, written in honor of the wedding of King Richard II of England to Anne of Bohemia in January 1382 – which, incidentally, turned out to be one of the most successful marriages of the era – he refers to the belief in the Middle Ages that February 14 marked the date when birds began to choose their mates.

> 'For this was on seynt Volantynys day
> Whan euery bryd comyth there to chese [choose]
> his make [mate].'
>
> **GEOFFREY CHAUCER**, *The Parliament of Fowls*

VALENTINE FACTS

In Wales, many people honor St. Dwynwen's Day on January 25 instead of or as well as St. Valentine's Day. St. Dwynwen is the patron saint of Welsh lovers.

Ancient tradition holds that if a young woman wants to know the identity of her future love, she can summon the appearance of her spouse-to-be by visiting a graveyard at midnight on the night before Valentine's Day. While running round the church twelve times, she has to sing a specific song, and then her lover will appear.

On Valentine's Day 2003, the popular Scottish wedding destination of Gretna Green set a new record by hosting the most weddings in a single day. Eighty-four couples – including lovebirds from as far afield as America, Jordan, Germany and Russia – exchanged vows there.

According to the Greeting Card Association, an estimated 1 billion Valentine cards are sent each year, making this day of lovers second only to Christmas as the biggest card-sending occasion of the year.

The First Valentine

Expressing one's love in the form of a written Valentine first occurred during the fifteenth century. Charles, Duke of Orléans, penned some of the early written Valentines. After his capture at the Battle of Agincourt in 1415, the duke was held captive in England until 1440. While there, he wrote dozens of love notes and impassioned verses to his wife, Bonne of Armagnac, who remained in France. Approximately sixty of these letters have survived the intervening years, and are held at the British Library in London.

O my Luve's like a red, red rose
That's newly sprung in June:
O my Luve's like the melodie,
That's sweetly play'd in tune.

ROBERT BURNS

The History of Valentine's Day

By the seventeenth century, the celebration of Valentine's Day was a well-established tradition across the world, not only for the exchange of cards and messages, but also of gifts.

In the early 1700s, Charles II of Sweden introduced to Europe the Persian art of the 'language of flowers': different meanings were attributed to different flowers, so that a hidden message could be expressed through a floral gift.

The red rose became symbolic of romantic love, which explains its enduring popularity to this day as a present for

♥♥♥♥♥♥♥♥♥♥♥♥♥♥♥♥♥♥♥♥♥♥♥♥♥♥♥♥♥♥♥♥♥♥♥♥♥

lovers: roughly 110 million roses (most of them red) are delivered on Valentine's Day each year.

The Language of Flowers

According to this ancient Persian art, flowers hold hidden meanings. Here are a handful of blooms associated with love, some with very specific messages:

Arbutus – 'Thee only do I love'
Red camellia – 'You're a flame in my heart'
Gardenia – 'You're lovely'
Heliotrope – for devotion
Lemon blossom – for fidelity
Mistletoe – 'Kiss me'
Pansy – 'I'm thinking of you'
Periwinkle – for sweet, pleasurable memories
Primrose – 'I can't live without you'
Spider flower – 'Elope with me'
Yellow irises – for passion

In addition to roses, orchids, myrtles, daisies, forget-me-nots, red chrysanthemums and red tulips all represent love. Gloxinia is said to mean 'love at first sight'.

Tip!

Why not ask your florist to make up a bouquet for your lover that spells out exactly how you feel? You might need to translate your message for your inamorata, though.

♥♥♥♥♥♥♥♥♥♥♥♥♥♥♥♥♥♥♥♥♥♥♥♥♥♥♥♥♥♥♥♥♥♥♥♥

ASIAN ARITHMETIC

Taiwanese tradition holds that the number of roses
sent to your lover conveys a particular message.
For example, one red rose equals 'an only love',
eleven roses mean 'a favorite', ninety-nine roses
say 'forever', and 108 roses ask 'marry me?'

Valentines Today

In modern times, Valentine's Day is still celebrated in all these traditional ways, but many lovers are put off by the overt commercialism of the day. However, this exploitation of love is nothing new – the first mass-produced Valentine cards emerged in early 1850s America, the brainchild of college graduate Esther Howland.

Valentine's Day doesn't have to be brutally commercial, though. It's a wonderful idea to have a day dedicated solely to your passion for your beloved, so take that premise and make your celebration of it something special just for the pair of you. Dinner in overpriced restaurants filled with tables for two, and life-sized cuddly bears dressed in T-shirts with the slogan 'Be My Valentine' are, after all, only optional accoutrements.

Let's Celebrate

Celebrating Valentine's Day is all about love and it should come from the heart. Here are some suggestions of personal ways to mark the day.

Heart-Shaped Goodness

You are what you eat: turn being consumed by love on its head and make your lover a host of eatables in the shape of a heart. The idea can be applied to your partner's favorite dishes: why not present them with a platter of heart-shaped Brie, or a steak or chicken breast carved into the ubiquitous symbol of love?

You can also buy heart-shaped cookie cutters and even heart-shaped poached-egg molds – the entire day can be filled with sculpted culinary creations, from breakfast to bedtime.

Here's a recipe for a heart-shaped cake with which to wow your lover.

Sweetheart's Sponge Cake

You will need:
For the sponge:
3 eggs
6 oz butter or margarine
6 oz self-raising flour
6 oz granulated sugar
packet of chocolate drops (optional)

For the butter cream filling and topping:
4 oz butter or margarine
8 oz granulated sugar

To decorate, choose from:
chocolate drops
loveheart sweets
fresh strawberries, cut into small pieces
glacé cherries
edible silver balls
other cake decorations of your choice

♥ ♥

Method:

1 Preheat the oven to 350°F.

2 Take two round cake pans, each measuring roughly 6.75 inches in diameter, and grease them or line with baking paper.

3 Using an electric whisk, mix together all the sponge ingredients in a large bowl.

4 Transfer the mixture to the cake pans in equal proportions.

5 Bake in the oven for 25 minutes, or until the sponge is springy to the touch. When they're cooked, turn out the sponges from the pans on to wire racks, and leave to cool.

6 Meanwhile, make the cream filling and topping by combining the butter or margarine and sugar together.

7 Once the cakes have cooled, place the sponges on top of each other. Using a sharp knife, cut round the sides to create a heart-shaped cake from the original circle. You may wish to use the lip of a mug as a stencil to help you create the curves at the top of the heart.

8 Momentarily separate the two sponges in order to spread the filling on the bottom half of the cake, then replace the other half and spread the remaining butter cream on top.

9 Decorate as desired: for example, by adding a trim to the edges of the cake; spelling out your loved one's name or both your initials (e.g. 'KG 4 DM'); writing 'I love you', 'Happy Valentine's Day' or another affectionate message; echoing the cake's shape by etching a smaller heart in its centre; or a combination of these.

♥ ♥

▼▼▼

Homemade Cards

Arts and crafts is a burgeoning industry, and you can now create gorgeous homemade cards that go way beyond the simplistic colored-pencil efforts of your youth. Furthermore, your lover is bound to cherish something you have made far more than any mass-produced, shop-bought article.

DECIDE ON YOUR DESIGN

This is the first step in creating a personalized Valentine. How would you like your card to look? You can get some inspiration from card shops and on card-making websites, or consider the elements below:

* Will you include a photograph of your loved one, the two of you together, or your favorite place?

* Would you like a layered effect, with multiple colored strips of card to embellish the design?

* If you're artistic, will you draw or paint a picture? Or would you prefer a text-based design, using words to express your feelings?

* Which colors look good together?

* Do you think a '3-D' effect – with items raised above the two-dimensional flat card – would suit your intentions? You can buy small foam pads from craft shops to achieve this découpage look.

* What shape of card do you want to make: something tall and thin, or square or round?

* If you like textured cards, think about gluing on ribbons, sequins, pressed flowers and other tactile objects.

▼▼▼

♥♥♥♥♥♥♥♥♥♥♥♥♥♥♥♥♥♥♥♥♥♥♥♥♥♥♥♥♥♥♥♥♥♥♥♥♥♥♥

HOW TO MAKE A HOMEMADE VALENTINE CARD

The best personalized cards are designed from the heart, so let your inspiration run wild when thinking up your own original card-making ideas. If you need a little help, though, here's a simple how-to guide for a homemade Valentine card to get you started. Don't forget that your card will only look as good as its raw materials, so don't stint on quality.

You will need:
1 piece stiff A4 black card
1 piece good quality A4 cream paper
1 small piece red card
23.5 inches red ribbon
(preferably of a hue to match the red card),
with a width of roughly 0.3 inch
pencil
glue
silver or gold glitter

Method:

1 Fold the black card in half to create a book-sized card (not a long, thin card). Work with the card in portrait rather than landscape mode, so that the longest sides of the card are vertical.

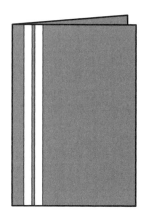

2 Cut two strips of ribbon that each measure the height of the card (roughly 8.25 inches). Glue one strip to the left-hand side of the card, approximately

♥♥♥♥♥♥♥♥♥♥♥♥♥♥♥♥♥♥♥♥♥♥♥♥♥♥♥♥♥♥♥♥♥♥♥♥♥♥♥

♥ ♥

0.4 inch from the edge. Glue the second strip to the first strip's right-hand side, leaving a 0.2 inch gap.

3 Using a pencil, draw a heart shape on the red card. The diameter of the heart at its widest point should be 1.75 inches. If you don't trust yourself to draw a heart freehand, use a stencil to help you.

4 Cut out the heart, and glue it to the middle of the black card, as measured from its right-hand edge to the ribbon edge.

5 Next, dab a little glue in the centre of the red heart, and sprinkle over the glitter. Stand the card upright immediately afterwards allowing the excess glitter to fall away.

6 Using the remaining ribbon, cut two strips of roughly 3 inches in length. Glue these on a diagonal angle in the top-right and bottom-right corners of the black card respectively. Trim off the excess ribbon at the sides.

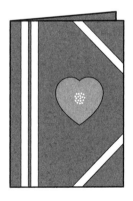

♥ ♥

7 Taking the sheet of cream paper, pencil in a border of 0.75 inch width from all four outer edges. Using this pencilled line as a guide, cut round it. Glue (or sew, see box below) the smaller-sized cream paper inside the black card.

TIP!

You could sew the cream paper to the black card, using a needle and some red thread.
Fold the cream paper in half before you begin to sew the two together and stitch up the seam of the folded black card, along the middle of the folded cream paper.

8 Once the glue has dried (or the stitching is complete), write your message on the cream paper.

'Love talked about can be easily turned aside, but love demonstrated is irresistible.'
W. STANLEY MOONEYHAM

The Language of Love

'I love you' are the three little words that mean so much. Why not strengthen their message by whispering the same sentiment to your partner in all the languages the world has to offer? Here are a few to start you off.

FRENCH
Je t'aime (juh tem)

GERMAN
Ich liebe dich
(ick leeber dick; 'ck' is pronounced
like the 'ch' in 'loch')

ITALIAN
Ti amo (tee ah-moh)

PORTUGUESE
Eu te amo (e-oo chee amoo)

SPANISH
Te amo (teh ah-moh)

SWEDISH
Jag älskar dig (yaag aelskar dey)

WELSH
Caru ti (cari tee)

♥♥♥♥♥♥♥♥♥♥♥♥♥♥♥♥♥♥♥♥♥♥♥♥♥♥♥♥♥♥♥♥♥♥♥♥

♥ ♥

British Sign Language

1 Use your index finger to point at your own chest.

2 Cross your hands over your chest.

3 Use your index finger to point at your partner.

Morse Code

This is useful for those situations, such as tea with the in-laws, where a non-verbal 'I love you' can come in handy. Just tap 'I love you' in Morse code on to your partner's hand, knee or arm and, unbeknownst to your parents, your lover will know exactly how you feel.

Give a stroke for a dash, and a quick squeeze for each dot.

I · ·

L · — · ·

O — — —

V · · · —

E ·

U · · —

'Married couples who love each other tell each other
a thousand things without talking.'
CHINESE PROVERB

♥ ♥

Baby, You're the Best

(or, actions guaranteed to sweep your lover off their feet – every time)

* Make your lover breakfast in bed (see pages 67–71 for tips on how to make it perfect)

* Slow dance together

* Organize a romantic surprise

* Keep an eye out for favored clothes fraying, lost jewelry, skipping CDs and damaged books – then provide replacements of their favorite things

* Give your partner a massage

* Cook their favorite meal

* Plan a day out or a weekend away together (see pages 76–81 for destination ideas)

* Make them a birthday cake (see pages 44–5 for a sponge cake recipe)

* Embrace them in a 'Hollywood' kiss – bend them backwards and swoop in for a snog

* Run them a warm bath (candles and scented bubble bath optional)

* Serenade your sweetheart

* Make them the first person you call whenever something exciting happens

Popping the Question

'It took great courage to ask a beautiful young woman to marry me. Believe me, it is easier to play the whole *Petrushka* on the piano.'

ARTHUR RUBINSTEIN

IT's one of the happiest – and for one of you, at least, the most nerve-wracking – days of a couple's life . . . and there's not an aisle in sight yet. Asking your loved one to marry you should perhaps be a simple affair: this person is your best friend and you want to spend the rest of your life with them, so what's the problem?

Factor in insecurity, commitment doubts, potential family nightmares to overcome, worries about the subsequent wedding planning (and spiraling costs), and the general pressures of organizing a proposal to blow all others out of the water – and it's surprising that anyone makes it far enough to say 'I do.'

Happily, love will out, and most people manage to get over all those wobbles in the end, as the following stories amply demonstrate.

In July 2007, John Dixon opted for a Hollywood-style proposal for his sweetheart, extreme sports fanatic Tamzin Davies. But don't think *Casablanca*, *Pretty Woman* or even *Jerry Maguire* – instead, think *Jaws*.

That's right – Mr. Dixon proposed in a shark tank, while the deadly creatures surrounded him and Tamzin. While they were

♥♥♥

underwater at the Blue Planet Aquarium in Cheshire, he whipped out a sign that read 'Marry me'. Tamzin later said: 'I just started crying.' But she still said yes.

> 'My most brilliant achievement was my ability to be able to persuade my wife to marry me.'
> **WINSTON CHURCHILL**

James Andrews knew for months in advance how he was going to propose to his girlfriend, Floss Allen. Enlisting his parents' help, he planned a dramatic entreaty in 164-foot-high letters. The backdrop? One of his parents' fields in Norwich.

Ahead of time, James roughly marked out the words with a Land Rover, before a cultivator etched them more deeply. Then, in August 2007 the lovers took to the skies, soaring over Norwich in a plane. When Floss saw the words – 'Floss, Marry Me?' – she said yes immediately.

> **PROPOSAL FACT**
> In 2004, Hollywood superstar George Clooney popped the question – again, and again, and again. A waxwork version of the acclaimed actor was on show at London tourist hotspot Madame Tussauds. Guests had a 'menu' of chat-up lines to try out on the famous bachelor, who offered candlelit dinners and marriage proposals in return.

♥♥♥♥♥♥♥♥♥♥♥♥♥♥♥♥♥♥♥♥♥♥♥♥♥♥♥♥♥♥♥♥♥♥♥♥♥♥♥

Dean Martin is better known as a singing sensation than a marital matchmaker, but for one lucky girl in the audience of *The Rat Pack Live from Las Vegas* at Blenheim Palace in July 2004, all that was to change.

Midway through the swing show, 'Dean Martin' – aka actor Mark Adams – stopped the performance to pop the question to Sarah Mason, on behalf of her boyfriend Stuart Crawley. She accepted his proposal in front of 5,000 people.

All together now: 'That's amore . . .'

SPELLBOUND

Deciding not to be outdone by outlandish modes of marriage proposals, seventy-five-year-old Pat West made an effort with her acceptance of Ernie Hubbard's proposition.

As the pair sat having alphabet spaghetti on toast for their tea, Ernie popped the question. In response, Pat kept him on the edge of his seat while she fished out the letters 'Y' 'E' 'S' in answer to his plea. The couple later married in November 2006.

In February 2003, Sunita Arora and Prakash Shah proved that great minds think alike when they both proposed to each other on Valentine's Day – by placing ads in national newspapers.

Prakash opted for *The Times*, where he asked his 'big fat-fatty bum wormy poo' to marry him; Sunita, meanwhile, made newspaper history with her ad when it became the first Valentine's Day advertisement to appear in the *Financial Times*.

♥♥♥♥♥♥♥♥♥♥♥♥♥♥♥♥♥♥♥♥♥♥♥♥♥♥♥♥♥♥♥♥♥♥♥♥♥♥♥

♥♥♥♥♥♥♥♥♥♥♥♥♥♥♥♥♥♥♥♥♥♥♥♥♥♥♥♥♥♥♥♥♥♥♥♥♥♥♥

Despite Prakash's outing of Sunita's, erm, affectionate nickname, they both accepted – in person.

'I'M NOT THE ONE YOU SHOULD BE ASKING . . .'

In summer 2007, a young man decided he was going to propose to his long-time girlfriend. He commissioned a unique ring design featuring two rubies and a diamond, planned the perfect setting and, as tradition dictates, approached his lover's mother (her father being deceased) to ask for her daughter's hand in marriage.

The mother gave her permission willingly, but just as the amorous suitor took his leave, she added: 'Of course, there's no guarantee that *she* will say yes.'

Happily, however, she did!

The Ring's the Thing

The giving of an engagement ring upon acceptance of a marriage proposal is a custom that stems from the old tradition of exchanging rings to seal a significant deal. In the Middle Ages, Italians believed that diamonds were created by the flames of love, which is why many modern engagement rings have a diamond as the central stone.

In Wales, men wishing to marry used to present their beloved with a hand-carved spoon rather than a ring. The tradition arose because lonely Welsh sailors would spend their

♥♥♥♥♥♥♥♥♥♥♥♥♥♥♥♥♥♥♥♥♥♥♥♥♥♥♥♥♥♥♥♥♥♥♥♥♥♥♥

♥♥♥♥♥♥♥♥♥♥♥♥♥♥♥♥♥♥♥♥♥♥♥♥♥♥♥♥♥♥♥♥♥♥♥♥♥♥

long hours at sea carving lovespoons for the partners they had been forced to leave behind. Spoons are still given as a sign of affection today.

ONCE UPON A TIME

For the Anglo-Saxon man, an engagement was an unknown commodity. When he wanted a lover, he just picked one, if necessary by kidnapping her from her father's home and taking her back to his place to make her clean, cook and bear children. All in all not the most romantic start to married life . . .

Love in a Leap Year

Every four years, an extra day is added to the calendar. That day is February 29, and the years in which it appears are termed 'leap years'. Tradition holds that because February 29 is such an unusual day, ordinary codes of conduct may be abandoned and customs turned on their head. Consequently, it's become famous as the day on which women can propose marriage.

Rumor has it that the tradition even became law: Queen Margaret of Scotland is said to have passed a 1288 statute that allowed women to propose to men throughout every leap year; not just on February 29. There were alleged penalties for men who refused such propositions, ranging from a fine of £1 to the purchase of a silk dress for the rejected lady.

♥♥♥♥♥♥♥♥♥♥♥♥♥♥♥♥♥♥♥♥♥♥♥♥♥♥♥♥♥♥♥♥♥♥♥♥♥♥

WILL YOU MARRY ME, MAN?

On February 29, 2000, Georgina Lewis both proposed to her surprised boyfriend – on TV – *and* married him. The unwitting groom-to-be, John O'Farrell, thought he and his girlfriend were appearing on ITV's *This Morning* to discuss an interior-design makeover for their home. Instead, Georgina took advantage of the unusual date to pop the question – and then, just three hours later, the couple got hitched at Southwark Register Office.

Sadie Hawkins Day

A different version of the leap-year tradition is Sadie Hawkins Day, which is traditionally honored in November. Many high schools host a Sadie Hawkins Dance, where the girls must ask the boys to be their date.

Sadie Hawkins was a character in Al Capp's cartoon strip *Li'l Abner*. In the strip, spinster Sadie's father organized a race for the townsfolk of Dogpatch, inviting all the single women in the town to chase the bachelors. The upshot was that any man caught had to wed the fleet-footed lady who had collared him.

First mentioned on November 13, 1937, Sadie Hawkins Day became an annual event in the strip, while dances and events associated with the cartoon character have since been held throughout America.

The Way to the Heart is Through the Stomach

> 'In love, as in gluttony,
> pleasure is a matter of the utmost precision.'
>
> **ITALO CALVINO**

THERE'S something about food that links it to love. Perhaps it's the sensuous nature of enjoying tastes. Maybe it's the aphrodisiac quality of certain nibbles. Or it could be the simple fact that, like love, we just can't live without it.

Top Ten Aphrodisiacs

Deriving from the Greek goddess of love, Aphrodite, an aphrodisiac is a food or drink that stimulates desire, so it's the perfect nourishment to serve your sweetheart.

You could consider including some of the following popular aphrodisiacs in your future recipes. To be extra specially romantic, why not name your new dish after your partner?

1. Asparagus
2. Avocados
3. Bananas
4. Carrots

⑤ Figs

⑥ Garlic

⑦ Ginger (the spice)

⑧ Oysters

⑨ Pine nuts

⑩ Chocolate*

*There's debate over whether or not this is a true aphrodisiac, but eating it definitely stimulates the pleasure areas in the brain, which can't be a bad thing!

Delicious Desserts

Most people have a sweet tooth that needs regular satisfaction, so preparing a delectable pudding for your lover is a sure-fire way to get in their good books.

The following simple yet stunning recipe is the ideal dessert to serve your lover, as it's perfect for a carefully planned evening of saucy seduction. Consequently it might be wise to leave it off a dinner-party menu, unless you're all *very* good friends . . .

Ice Cream and Hot Chocolate Liqueur Sauce

SERVES FOUR
You will need:
75 g (3 oz) plain chocolate or cooking chocolate
200 ml (7 fl oz) cold water
2 tsp custard powder or cornflour
1 tbsp Cointreau or Grand Marnier liqueur
1 level tbsp granulated sugar
vanilla ice cream

♥ ♥

♥ ♥

Method:

1. Break the chocolate up into squares and put into a mixing bowl that fits just above a pan of simmering water. Add 2 tbsp cold water to the chocolate pieces and heat over the water, stirring occasionally until the chocolate melts.

2. Then, beat the chocolate mix until smooth, gradually adding 7 fl oz water.

3. Mix the custard powder or cornflour with 30 ml (2 tbsp) water in a cup, then stir into the chocolate sauce in the bowl and heat gently over the pan for 3–4 minutes. Next, stir in the liqueur and the sugar.

4. Leave until just before serving. To reheat, give it a quick blast in the microwave or bring the water back to the boil and stir the sauce until it is hot.

5. Serve the ice cream in bowls and pour a generous helping of the hot sauce on top.

'I cook with wine – sometimes I even add it to the food.'

W. C. FIELDS

Melt Your Lover's Heart

Another fantastic food idea for lovers is fondue: cheese if your partner favors savouries, and chocolate for the sweet-toothed sweetheart.

Glory in the tactile nature of eating fondue – feeding each other is practically compulsory. Nibbles to dip into a gooey chocolate mix include fresh fruit, marshmallows and brioche,

♥ ♥

while crudités and slices of French stick can be dropped into melted *fromage*.

A DESSERT WITH A DIFFERENCE

On Valentine's Day 2002, one young lady didn't get quite what she ordered. Dining with her boyfriend in the restaurant where they'd had their first date, she selected a tasty pudding from the menu and waited for it to arrive.

But instead of crème brûlée, what should appear but a cake. And what should be iced upon the cake but 'Will You Marry Me?' And what should be sparkling in its center but a diamond engagement ring . . .

How to Prepare the Perfect Picnic

Hot summer days bring out the best in romantics. There's no better weather in which to pack up a hamper full of delicious treats, drive out to the country, seaside or nearest park – with the windows down, your favorite songs blaring on the stereo and your hand on your lover's knee – spread out a tartan blanket in a shady, picturesque spot, and feed each other finger food from a selection of delectable eats. Heaven.

If the weather lets you down and the sun refuses to shine, prepare an indoor picnic instead: lay out that blanket on your bedroom or living-room floor, recline on your elbows as you would in a verdant field, and relish the unconventionality of picnicking in your own home.

♥♥♥♥♥♥♥♥♥♥♥♥♥♥♥♥♥♥♥♥♥♥♥♥♥♥♥♥♥♥♥♥♥♥♥♥♥

Here's One I Made Earlier

To host the perfect picnic, advance preparation and forethought are key. Before you head for the hills with your hamper . . .

* Prepare as much of the food as you can, so that it's ready to eat as soon as you sit down. So, chop the crudités, bake and chill the quiches, assemble the salads and make the sandwiches before you set off for the Great Outdoors.

* Ensure any ice blocks for the cool bag are completely frozen, so that the food and drinks are kept chilled on the journey. Make sure you pop them in the freezer the night before.

* Pack the hamper thoughtfully, working out what you'll need for each meal. Forks, plates, plastic cups and paper napkins are standard, but you might also need teaspoons for dessert, a corkscrew for the wine, a spare plastic bag for rubbish/dirty crockery, a sharp knife and other paraphernalia. Don't forget the tablecloth or blanket, too.

* Safety first: you might want to slip some sun cream and insect repellent into the bag on hot summer days. A hat and shades would also be handy.

* Location, location, location. You may wish to choose the perfect picnic spot before you take your partner there.

Finger Food

The perfect picnic food doesn't require a full dinner service in order to eat it. Nibbles should be bite-sized and easily transported, either as they are or in plastic containers. Here are a few portable suggestions:

♥▼♥▼♥▼♥▼♥▼♥▼♥▼♥▼♥▼♥▼♥▼♥▼♥▼♥▼♥▼♥▼♥▼♥▼♥▼♥

✳ cherry tomatoes

✳ carrot sticks

✳ pre-chopped celery sticks, pre-sliced peppers
and precut cucumber sticks

✳ dips such as houmous, tzatsiki, taramasalata and salsa

✳ mini quiches

✳ cold new potatoes, pre-cooked with sprigs of rosemary
and sprinkled with rock salt

✳ French bread or savoury biscuits, served with cheeses
like Brie and Le Roulé

✳ pre-prepared salads: potato; lentil; Greek; pasta;
coleslaw; rice; couscous

✳ premade sandwiches, rolls and mini pitas,
all cut in half for ease of consumption – fillings
could include: cheese and ham; roast chicken slices
with cranberry sauce; pâté; pesto, mozzarella
and tomato; Brie and apple; BLT

✳ cocktail sausages

✳ chicken drumsticks

✳ crisps and nuts

Don't forget dessert:

✳ chocolate brownies

✳ individual chocolate mousses

✳ bunches of seedless grapes

✳ fresh strawberries

✳ cherries

TIP!

A bright and colorful picnic looks best on a picnic plate. Think about the colors and textures of the foods you're serving, and ensure you've got a good, varied range, with bright reds, yellows and greens all present and correct.

Bottoms up:

* champagne
* individual cartons of fruit juice (with straws)
* chilled white or rosé wine
* premade Pimms and lemonade
* freshly squeezed fruit juices

THIS LITTLE LOVER WENT TO MARKET

Why not combine your picnic with a trip to your local farmers' market? You can pick up the freshest, tastiest produce while also enjoying a romantic stroll around the tempting stalls, hand in hand with your lover.

Cocktails for Couples

Head over Heels, Silk Stocking, Slippery Nipple, Sex on the Beach, Screaming Orgasm . . . and not necessarily in that order.

♥ ♥

Cocktails have always been rather provocatively named, and the heady combinations of their main ingredients are no less sensuous than their titles suggest.

Why not stock up the drinks cabinet, invest in a shaker and strainer, and host your own cocktail evening, just for you and your partner? Turn the lights down low, put some piano jazz on the stereo and dress to impress.

Who knows where the night could end, given some of these outrageous tipples? But in the meantime a great place to start is with a Kiss in the Dark.

Kiss in the Dark Cocktail

SERVES TWO
You will need:
2 shots gin
2 shots dry vermouth
2 shots cherry brandy
8 ice cubes
1 cocktail shaker
1 strainer
2 cocktail glasses

Method:

1 Put all the ingredients in a cocktail shaker, and shake well.

2 Using the strainer, pour the mixture into the cocktail glasses.

3 Decorate with paper umbrellas, sparklers, plastic monkeys and slices of fruit according to taste (or otherwise).

4 Serve immediately.

♥ ♥

♥▾

How to Make the Perfect Breakfast in Bed

'I love romance: I bring Keely breakfast in bed on a tray
with a single flower from our garden. I did that when
we first started dating, and I still do it.'

PIERCE BROSNAN

Breakfast in bed is the perfect way to indulge your lover. While
they recline in the comfort of their king-size, propped up with
pillows and with the still-warm duvet tucked around their legs,
you can attend to their every need, bringing hot toast and tea
on demand, and enjoying their gorgeous laziness by proxy. But
how do you prepare the perfect breakfast in bed?

Step One: Timing is Everything

Don't limit yourself to the established special occasions to treat
your partner in this way – while birthdays, anniversaries,
Valentine's Day, and so on will all set the scene for this early-
morning indulgence, why not surprise your lover every now and
then with some spontaneous generosity?

Choose your moment carefully. It's all very well planning to
wake them with a kiss, à la Sleeping Beauty, but if your partner
is the sort who needs their beauty sleep, it could all end
grumpily. If you're an early riser who has usually completed a
couple of triathlons before dawn, but your lover is not, wait
until their normal waking hours before you burst into the bedroom with a rose between your teeth and a tray balanced
carefully on one arm.

♥▾

Bear in mind it works both ways, too – so if your lover is normally up with the birds, you'll have to get up even earlier simply to catch them in bed with your lovingly prepared *petit déjeuner*.

> The classic soul song 'Breakfast in Bed' was a hit for Dusty Springfield in 1969 and for UB40 in 1988, as well as several other artists over the years.

Step Two: The Menu

It goes without saying that the perfect breakfast in bed is the one tailored to your partner's taste buds. A vegetarian won't look too kindly on even the freshest smoked-salmon-and-cream-cheese bagel, and a teetotaller won't be swept away by champagne. Similarly, it would seem foolish to serve summer foods in the heart of winter, and vice versa.

Decide in advance what you're going to prepare, how many 'courses' there may be, and whether your lover would like a light bite or a full English. Here are some suggestions for inspiration.

Food ideas:

✳ fresh fruit (grapefruit/strawberries/
a seasonal selection)

✳ cereal/porridge

✳ Greek yogurt with honey and nuts

✳ traditional toast spread with butter, jam,
honey or Marmite

✳ toasted bagels with smoked salmon and cream cheese

❤ ❤

✻ scrambled eggs

✻ boiled eggs with toast soldiers

✻ full English breakfast with bacon, sausage, egg,
hash browns, baked beans, tomatoes and mushrooms

✻ waffles with maple syrup

✻ your partner's favorite food,
whether it's breakfast fare or not

Drink ideas:

✻ champagne

✻ Bucks Fizz (shop bought or 'homemade assembly'
by the bedside – the latter enables you
to achieve your partner's preferred
juice-to-booze ratio)

✻ fresh fruit smoothie

✻ freshly squeezed fruit juice

✻ tea

✻ coffee

✻ hot chocolate (whipped cream on top optional)

Step Three: The Flourishes

Don't forget those little details that make it more than just an
ordinary breakfast:

✻ A flower on the tray is a nice touch. There may not be
space for an actual vase, so don't be afraid to place a
single stem alongside the plate or to bring in an entire
bouquet – after you've presented the tray – and arrange
it so that your partner can see the flowers as they eat.

❤ ❤

✿ If the breakfast is a true surprise, you may wish to keep the food under wraps until the last possible moment, so cover the dish until you're ready to make a dramatic revelation of the delicacies on offer.

✿ A gentle soundtrack can make a world of difference to the moment. Set up the CD player ahead of your entrance, and your music choice will set the mood perfectly.

✿ Consider the impact of the breakfast tray itself. Your best crockery and a champagne flute set off by a linen napkin is an immediate indication of the effort to which you've gone. To be really fancy, you could tie colored ribbons to the tray's handles, but check they don't trail in the food . . .

✿ You might include a little gift for your lover – that morning's newspaper or a trinket you've seen that you know they'd like or a love poem that you've written yourself (see pages 146–9 for advice on how to write one).

TIP!

Check your sleepy sweetheart is ready for a sudden influx of light, then open the curtains wide to let in the brand-new day you're about to enjoy together. There's nothing nicer than seeing a bright blue sky or snow-covered roofs from your window. Alternatively, maintain the slumberous ambience with cozy bedside lamps, fairy lights or candles.

Step Four: Don't Leave Your Lover Lonely

If you're not eating too, simply curl up on the bed next to your loved one and share a breakfast drink. Toast each other's happiness. This is not the time to be worrying about the washing-up or the leaving of crumbs in the sheets.

MESSAGE IN A MARGARINE TUB

Food brought one very happy couple together during the Second World War. One day, single sixteen-year-old Bette Kennedy was hard at work at the Co-op margarine factory in Irlam near Manchester, when she decided to entrust her romantic destiny to fate. Clandestinely, she slipped her name and address into a margarine tub bound for British forces.

The tub was found by a ship's cook, who persuaded Herbie Reynolds, the minesweeper's only bachelor sailor, to make contact with the mystery margarine lass. After corresponding for a while, the pair met in Portsmouth – and fell deeply in love. They married in 1946.

Mr. Reynolds later said: 'It was a million-to-one chance that Bette's message found me. Maybe it was fate, but I was a very lucky man.'

The couple have now been married for over sixty years, and have five children, fifteen grandchildren and twenty great-grandchildren.

Love on the Silver Screen

MOVIES have always captured the romantic imagination. In 2004, the Royal Society of Chemistry published a list of the top screen couples who, in their opinion, had generated the most chemistry in celluloid history. Here's their top three:

Spencer Tracy and Katharine Hepburn

This real-life couple topped the chart. They starred in nine films together, from the 1942 movie *Woman of the Year* to *Guess Who's Coming to Dinner?* in 1967.

Their off-screen relationship was just as successful, lasting almost three decades before Tracy's death in June 1967 (poignantly, he died just seventeen days after filming on their last movie together was completed).

Richard Burton and Elizabeth Taylor

Another off-screen couple who positively sizzled on celluloid, Burton and Taylor are perhaps best remembered for the 1963 movie megalith *Cleopatra* (see pages 17–19 for more detail on the besotted Queen of Egypt), as well as the brutal depiction of a turbulent marriage in *Who's Afraid of Virginia Woolf?* The two were also married twice (and divorced twice); a testament to their fiery relationship.

♥♥

'Cupid's dart had hit both targets and set the Nile on fire. And the Tiber. Even the Thames sizzled a bit.'

People magazine on the occasion of Burton's death, recalling Burton and Taylor's real-life romance while they were filming *Cleopatra*

Humphrey Bogart and Lauren Bacall

Bogart and Bacall were first paired in the 1944 movie adaptation of Hemingway's novel *To Have and Have Not*. Bacall's infamous line is often quoted: 'You know how to whistle, don't you, Steve? Just put your lips together . . . and blow.'

Sensationally, forty-five-year-old Bogart divorced his wife to marry the young Lauren, who was nineteen when they began filming. It was a long-lasting, happy relationship, which produced two children and endured until Bogart's death in January 1957. The duo also starred in the tour de force *The Big Sleep*, as well as *Dark Passage* and *Key Largo*.

QUEEN MEG

For many, actress Meg Ryan is the queen bee of romantic comedy films, particularly those made in the 1990s. Indeed she starred in four of the top-twenty most romantic films, as determined by Dream Date. Her hits include *Sleepless in Seattle*, with Tom Hanks; *When Harry Met Sally*, with Billy Crystal; *City of Angels*, with Nicolas Cage; and *You've Got Mail*, again with Hanks.

♥ ♥

Top Ten Romantic Films

Online dating agency Dream Date surveyed over 1,000 people to find the most romantic movies of all time. Here are their results, recommending the perfect movies to watch while cuddled up to your loved one on the sofa.

1. *Sleepless in Seattle* (1993)

2. *Titanic* (1997)

3. *Gone with the Wind* (1939)

4. *Casablanca* (1942)

5. *Pretty Woman* (1990)

6. *When Harry Met Sally* (1989)

7. *Ghost* (1990)

8. *An Affair to Remember* (1957)

9. *Romeo and Juliet* (1968 and 1996)

10. *City of Angels* (1998)

Film Facts

Burt Lancaster and Deborah Kerr's clinch in *From Here to Eternity* (1953) topped a 2007 poll to find the most memorable movie kiss. Richard Gere's finale efforts with Debra Winger in *An Officer and a Gentleman* (1982) came third, while the spaghetti smooching dogs in Disney's *Lady and the Tramp* (1955) took second place.

♥ ♥

♥♥♥♥♥♥♥♥♥♥♥♥♥♥♥♥♥♥♥♥♥♥♥♥♥♥♥♥♥♥♥♥♥♥♥♥♥

Hollywood marriages get bad press, but there are some success stories. The prize for the longest Hollywood marriage goes to Bob Hope and Dolores DeFina. On their wedding day in February 1934, few would have guessed that they would go on to enjoy sixty-nine years of married life together, which ended with Bob's death in July 2003.

There's debate over the length of the longest on-screen kiss. Some say the 1941 movie *You're in the Army Now*, starring Regis Toomey and Jane Wyman, takes the prize with a smooch of three minutes and five seconds; others that the 2005 film *Kids in America* trumped that with a kiss between Gregory Smith and Stephanie Sherrin that lasted over six minutes: rival records sources list both.

Famous Love Quotes from the Movies

'Love means never having to say you're sorry.'
Love Story (1970)

'[Love is] to be two and at the same time one.'
The Hunchback of Notre Dame (1939)

'I love you. I've loved you since the first moment I saw you.
I guess maybe I even loved you before I saw you.'
A Place in the Sun (1951)

♥♥♥♥♥♥♥♥♥♥♥♥♥♥♥♥♥♥♥♥♥♥♥♥♥♥♥♥♥♥♥♥♥♥♥♥♥♥♥

Mini-Break Magic

A WEEKEND away with your lover is the pinnacle of couple-dom. The opportunities for romance are endless: springing a surprise trip; having champagne already chilling in the hotel on arrival; getting a street artist to draw your lover . . .

Above all, a mini-break is a chance for the two of you to indulge in the best of activities: simply being together. Although your love alone guarantees you a fantastic getaway, wherever you're headed, here's a rundown of some of the world's most romantic destinations, along with tips on the best ways to spend your time there (providing you make it out of the hotel room, that is).

Paris

Renowned as perhaps the most romantic city on the planet, the capital of France has much to offer holidaying paramours.

Meander the charming streets of Montmartre, populated by street artists and dominated by the impressive white-domed *Basilique du Sacré-Cœur*; take a boat cruise along the Seine; and sample the regional delicacies on offer at the Rue Mouffetard morning market.

You could visit Île Saint-Louis, a tiny island secreted away on the Seine itself, with its cafés, ice-cream parlors and shops: a tranquil oasis right at the heart of the city.

No trip to Paris should exclude its art galleries – visit the *Venus de Milo*, the famous statue of the goddess of love at the Musée du Louvre, or the delights of Rodin's museum, which include a marble version of his statue *The Kiss* (see page 107).

By night, take a stroll by the Eiffel Tower, which will stand floodlit and glorious against the Parisian night sky.

'In the movies, Paris is designed as a backdrop for only three things – love, fashion shows, and revolution.'

JEANINE BASINGER

Santorini

This dramatic Grecian isle has been a popular destination for honeymooners and amorous visitors for decades.

On the site of a caldera – a large volcanic crater – Santorini rises from the Aegean Sea in scattered pieces, having long ago been blown apart by the smoldering, still active volcano located a short distance away. Out of all this devastating volcanic activity lies a small island of stunning physical beauty, and host to some of the world's most breathtaking views.

Visit the capital, Fira, for the best views over the caldera. It's a picturesque town full of whitewashed buildings with bright blue-domed roofs; you can find hidden delights away from the crowds only moments from the tourist traps.

The town of Oia, meanwhile, boasts the best sunsets on Santorini. Wind your way through its narrow streets to emerge with a spectacular view of the ocean and the slowly setting sun.

> If traveling the world isn't your thing or within your budget (or you just fancy a retreat in your home country), think about hiring a cozy cottage in the middle of nowhere for the weekend. Or you could rent a VW camper van and take a road trip to wherever you please: just the two of you, the open road and your dreams.

Venice

Venice was once described by *Time Out* as: 'A unique urban masterpiece [with] canals instead of streets, boats instead of buses, and ornate bridges instead of subways.' No trip to this magical place would be complete without a gondola ride from the Rialto Bridge down the Grand Canal, accompanied by a sweet serenade from your gondolier.

Make sure you seek out the famous Bridge of Sighs, too – tradition holds that if you kiss beneath the bridge at sunset, you're assured eternal love together.

Alternatively, explore the maze of backstreets on foot. You can find your way by using Venice's many churches as a point of reference, but otherwise lose yourselves in some of Italy's most inspiring architecture, as you stroll hand in hand through a uniquely beautiful city.

♥♥♥♥♥♥♥♥♥♥♥♥♥♥♥♥♥♥♥♥♥♥♥♥♥♥♥♥♥♥♥♥♥♥♥♥♥♥♥

A visit in the spring could see you become a part of the famous Venetian carnival, celebrated in honor of Mardi Gras. Masked romance beckons!

'A realist, in Venice, would become a romantic, by mere faithfulness to what he saw before him.'

ARTHUR SYMONS

New York

The Big Apple will be familiar to romantics as the backdrop to so many slushy movies. *Sleepless in Seattle* reached its climax at the top of the Empire State Building – one of the most swoonsome spots in the city. Why not reenact your favorite filmic moments around New York, New York?

You could also take a horse-drawn carriage ride around Central Park, shop at Tiffany's on Fifth Avenue, visit the city's many excellent museums, or try to skate like Torvill and Dean on the ice rink at the Rockefeller Center. Triple axels optional.

By night, dine in style on a boat cruise, taking in the many sights on the Manhattan skyline to the accompaniment of a trio of acoustic musicians.

Sydney

Perhaps Australia's most famous city, Sydney certainly lives up to its reputation as a dream location for lovers. For a start, there's a lot less light pollution than in other cities, which makes this the ideal place for some soulful stargazing. Check out Observatory Park and the Sydney Observatory for some awe-inspiring sights.

One of Sydney's top attractions is, of course, its Opera House, the centerpiece of one of the most recognizable vistas on the planet. An aria or two in an evening show could be just the thing to make both your hearts sing. Or you could set your lover's pulse racing by taking a thirty-minute seaplane flight from the spectacular Sydney Harbour to Cottage Point, near Pittwater. Take in the dramatic sights of the Opera House and Bondi Beach by air, before landing at an intimate waterside restaurant for lunch.

Other romantic treats on offer in the city include High Tea at the Victoria Room in Darlinghurst, and pre-dinner aperitifs in the bars off Bondi Beach.

Further Inspiration

Here are ten more locations renowned for romance. Where will the pair of you go next?

1. Quebec City, Canada
2. Boise, Idaho
3. Florence, Italy
4. Grenada, Spain
5. Lisbon, Portugal
6. London, England
7. Moscow, Russia
8. Prague, Czech Republic
9. Rome, Italy
10. Vienna, Austria

Yes, Let's!

Why not take inspiration from this drama improvization game when planning holidays and day trips? The rules of the game are that whenever someone suggests an activity – no matter how crazy, foolish or fantastic – the other person has to reply: 'Yes, let's!' And then you both embark on the proposed adventure. Who knows what you may find yourselves doing . . .

Day Tripping

Sometimes, it's impossible to squeeze in a mini-break when you've both got social commitments booked in the diary every weekend until Christmas, for instance . . . and it's only July.

Fear not, though, for you can still get your fix of escapist romance. Just shorten the schedule to a full day out. Throw yourselves into it with gusto, pack in lunches and strolls and casual kisses, and you'll find yourselves almost as refreshed and loved up as if you'd taken some proper time out. How about . . .

* a drive in the countryside

* a day at a theme park

* a tour round all the points of interest in the town where you live (that you've never gone to see before)

* a sashay to the seaside

* a trip to a nearby city

Love in Literature

LOVE is the great inspiration for writers, from chick lit to literary masterpieces. Though the classic works often end in tragedy, the passions driving their narratives have endured through time, regardless (or perhaps because) of the subjects' calamitous fates.

Whether or not they get a happy ending, the following famous lovers from literature are simply unforgettable.

Romeo and Juliet

The most famous fictional lovers of all time, Romeo and Juliet are the eponymous heroes of Shakespeare's late-sixteenth-century play (and Italian stories before that). Their narrative has always resonated with people, as the countless operas, ballets, songs and films associated with the pair attest.

Their story is this. The Montagues and Capulets, two rival families, have long been at each other's throats. When the teenage Romeo Montague and Juliet Capulet fall in love, an optimistic friar secretly marries them in the hope that it will end the feud. But fate intervenes, the lovers are forced to separate, and a plan is set in motion with inexorable consequences. *Romeo and Juliet* describes a love that is rent apart by family conflict, but ultimately united in death.

Although Shakespeare's play is a tragedy, its poetry and passion have made it a must-read (and must-see) for lovers throughout the ages, as the following beautiful extract illuminates, recalling the desperate attempts we've all made to deny that it is time to leave our loved ones when morning comes.

JULIET: Wilt thou be gone? It is not yet near day:
It was the nightingale, and not the lark,
That pierc'd the fearful hollow of thine ear;
Nightly she sings on yon pomegranate tree:
Believe me, love, it was the nightingale.
[. . .]

ROMEO: I am content, so thou wilt have it so.
I'll say yon grey is not the morning's eye,
'Tis but the pale reflex of Cynthia's brow;
Nor that is not the lark whose notes do beat
The vaulty heaven so high above our heads:
I have more care to stay than will to go.

Romeo and Juliet, Act III, Scene v

SHAKESPEARE ON SCREEN

The iconic story of the star-cross'd lovers has inspired
both straightforward adaptations and spin-offs.
The many film versions of *Romeo and Juliet* include:

West Side Story (1961)

Romeo and Juliet (1968, directed by Franco Zeffirelli)

Romeo + Juliet (1996, directed by Baz Luhrmann)

Shakespeare in Love (1998)

Romeo Must Die (2000)

High School Musical (2006)

▼▼▼▼▼▼▼▼▼▼▼▼▼▼▼▼▼▼▼▼▼▼▼▼▼▼▼▼▼▼▼▼▼▼▼

'An archaeologist is the best husband any woman can have: the older she gets, the more interested he is in her.'

AGATHA CHRISTIE

Sheherazade and King Shahryar

Arabian Nights is a storytelling tour de force, comprising a supposed 1,001 stories, mostly evolved from Persian, Arab and Indian tales. The framing device that contains these legends describes these famous lovers.

Once upon a time, the wife of King Shahryar made the grave mistake of betraying him. Her punishment was to be executed posthaste, but such drastic action wasn't enough to satisfy the enraged king. Chillingly, he determined to make the whole of womankind pay for his wife's crime. Every day, he married a young girl, spent the night with her, and then had her beheaded at sunrise.

One day, this unhappy fate fell to the intelligent Sheherazade. Keen to avoid her looming execution, she used her night with the king to tell a tale – a story that stopped on a cliffhanger come morning. Desperate to know what happened next, Shahryar postponed Sheherazade's beheading for a day, so that he could hear the ending.

But the next night, after quickly completing the first tale, Sheherazade spent the next few hours spinning another story: again, she stopped just before the climax, as the sun rose in the sky. Once again, the execution was postponed.

▼▼▼▼▼▼▼▼▼▼▼▼▼▼▼▼▼▼▼▼▼▼▼▼▼▼▼▼▼▼▼▼▼▼▼

▼▼▼

Famously, the wily bride kept this up for 1,001 nights – after which time, the king declared his true passion for her, spared her life, and they lived happily ever after.

Jane Eyre and Edward Rochester

Charlotte Brontë's romantic tale of a young governess and her erstwhile employer has entranced readers for generations. First published in 1847, *Jane Eyre*'s narrator is the young Jane herself, a plain but clever orphan, who first encounters the foreboding Edward Rochester when she accepts a teaching post at his home, Thornfield Hall.

At first, she finds him distant and daunting, but over time her feelings change. However, a dark secret threatens their happiness, and both must endure separation and betrayal before the truth will out. Theirs is a love that transcends physicality, speaks of soulmates, and demands fulfilment, even in the face of many obstacles.

> I know what it is to live entirely for and with what I love best on earth. [. . .] No woman was ever nearer to her mate than I am: ever more absolutely bone of his bone and flesh of his flesh. I know no weariness of my Edward's society: he knows none of mine [. . .] consequently, we are ever together. To be together is for us to be at once as free as in solitude, as gay as in company.
>
> *Jane Eyre*

▼▼▼

♥♥

Marguerite and Armando

The love story of Marguerite and Armando, as told in Alexandre Dumas's novel *La Dame aux Camélias*, and later adapted for the stage as *Camille*, is widely thought to be based on the playwright's real-life relationship.

When the courtesan Marguerite Gautier and the distinguished Armando Duval fall desperately in love, their happiness is complete. But Armando's father is less impressed by the scandalous affair, fearing it will ruin his son's prospects. He visits Marguerite and, after much pressure, persuades her to abandon her love.

In time, the noble courtesan becomes gravely ill. Again, Armando's father visits her, but this time he realizes the true depth of her feelings for his son. He vows to send Armando to her. Although he keeps his promise, he is too late: by the time Armando reaches his love, she is on the brink of death from tuberculosis, and all too soon the lovers are parted.

Elizabeth Bennet and Mr. Darcy

Jane Austen's *Pride and Prejudice* is frequently voted as one of readers' favorite books of all time. Its main protagonists are Elizabeth Bennet, the sensible second daughter of five in the Bennet family, and Fitzwilliam Darcy, a seemingly arrogant gentleman, and a friend of Charles Bingley, another gentleman, who rents a property close to the Bennets' home – thus setting both the Bennets' marriage-hungry mother into paroxysms of excitement, and the plot into motion.

♥♥

After many complex twists and turns, fueled by misunderstandings, lies and hidden motives, not to mention confused morals and not a few marriage matches, the heroes finally realize their true love for one another, and eventually tie the knot.

MR. DARCY!

The 1995 BBC TV miniseries of Austen's classic starred Colin Firth as Mr. Darcy and Jennifer Ehle as Elizabeth. It's particularly famous for a scene where Darcy, dripping wet, walks out of a lake, and is spotted by a rather flustered Miss Bennet.

Cathy and Heathcliff

The lovers from Emily Brontë's sweeping epic *Wuthering Heights* have proved enduringly popular, inspiring a host of pop songs, musicals, operas and modern literary updates since first publication in 1847.

Heathcliff is an orphan who is rescued by Mr. Earnshaw and taken into his home, Wuthering Heights, to be brought up alongside his children, Cathy and Hindley. Cathy and Heathcliff soon become inseparable companions. But when Mr. Earnshaw dies and Hindley inherits the Heights, he forces Heathcliff to become a lowly laborer, rather than the equal of his sister. In time, Cathy marries Edgar Linton, a far more 'suitable' husband, but her feelings for Heathcliff still rule her heart. When she dies in childbirth soon after, Heathcliff, driven mad by love and grief, begs her spirit to haunt him.

Set on the Yorkshire moors, the novel describes a wild love that is echoed in the harsh geographical setting: a love that has little to do with convention or morals, and everything to do with passion.

> My love for Heathcliff resembles the eternal rocks beneath – a source of little visible delight, but necessary. Nelly, I am Heathcliff! He's always, always in my mind – not as a pleasure, any more than I am always a pleasure to myself, but as my own being.
>
> *Wuthering Heights*

Top Ten Most Romantic Novels

Since 1960, the Romantic Novelists' Association in the UK has awarded a prize to the best romantic novel of the year. The winners from the past ten years are listed below. Each would make a great romantic gift for your lover, or you could try to hunt down a first or early edition of their favorite book, now or from childhood.

2007 – *Iris & Ruby* by Rosie Thomas

2006 – *Gardens of Delight* by Erica James

2005 – *A Good Voyage* by Katharine Davies

2004 – *Foreign Fruit* by Jojo Moyes

2003 – *Playing James* by Sarah Mason

♥♥

♥ ♥

2002 – *The Other Boleyn Girl* by Philippa Gregory

2001 – *Someone Like You* by Cathy Kelly

2000 – *Dancing in the Dark* by Maureen Lee

1999 – *Learning to Swim* by Clare Chambers

1998 – *Kiss and Kin* by Angela Lambert

BOOK CLUB FOR TWO

Why not start a couple's book club?
No other members necessary.

It doesn't have to be formal. Every time you read a great book that you think your partner would love, simply give them a copy to read.

When they've read it, have a good old chat about your respective thoughts and reactions to the text. You might be surprised to learn what your lover liked and disliked about the book.

♥ ♥

The Happiest Day of Your Lives

As Abba once put it, rather emphatically: 'I do, I do, I do, I do, I do.' A couple's wedding day is a wonderful celebration of two lovers' affection for, commitment to and delight in one another. What could be better than declaring your passion for your beloved, and formally embarking on the rest of your lives together? Bliss. Plus, you can have a big party with all of your closest friends.

This chapter celebrates all things wedding, from ancient traditions to unusual ways of tying the knot.

Back in the Day: Wedding Traditions

According to the ancient Greek historian Herodotus, the wedding rituals of the Nasamones of Libya compelled the bride to have sex with all the men attending the official ceremony.

▼▼▼▼▼▼▼▼▼▼▼▼▼▼▼▼▼▼▼▼▼▼▼▼▼▼▼▼▼▼▼▼

Sources suggest that a best man's role used to be part-bouncer, part-bodyguard. At the groom's request, he was on hand to defend the wedding party in case any rival suitors gatecrashed the do, or there were any other disturbances. Sounds a bit more hard core than simply having to remember the rings!

It was once believed by the ancient Greeks that the third finger on the left hand linked directly to the heart – which is why we wear our wedding rings on that very digit.

> 'I think men who have a pierced ear are better prepared for marriage. They've experienced pain and bought jewelry.'
>
> **RITA RUDNER**

Every Saturday in the summer, church bells ring out regularly, thus signifying that another wedding has taken place. The bell-ringing isn't just a joyful expression of the blessed day, however, as in times past it was executed to scare away evil spirits that might threaten the couple's future happiness.

The throwing of the bridal bouquet was once a form of self-protection. A tradition had evolved whereby wedding guests would tear off pieces of the bride's dress for good luck. In order

▼▼▼▼▼▼▼▼▼▼▼▼▼▼▼▼▼▼▼▼▼▼▼▼▼▼▼▼▼▼▼▼

to get away from the pursuing mob, the bride would chuck her bouquet at them and make a run for it.

These days, of course, the tradition is that the person who catches the bouquet will be the next to marry.

The custom of the wedding breakfast first arose in Roman times, when a marriage was not legal until the bride and groom had broken bread together.

When to Wed?

In modern times, Saturday is the most popular day to get married. Yet in the past it was considered an ill-fated day to hold a wedding, as this ancient rhyme shows:

> Monday for wealth,
> Tuesday for health,
> Wednesday the best day of all.
> Thursday for losses,
> Friday for crosses,
> Saturday for no luck at all.

There was also a ditty to describe the months of the year and their impact on a marriage's future:

> Married when the year is new, he'll be loving, kind and true.
> When February birds do mate, you wed nor dread your fate.
> If you wed when March winds blow, joy and sorrow both you'll know.
> Marry in April when you can, joy for maiden and for man.
> Marry in the month of May, and you'll surely rue the day.

♥ ♥

♥♥♥♥♥♥♥♥♥♥♥♥♥♥♥♥♥♥♥♥♥♥♥♥♥♥♥♥♥♥♥♥♥♥♥

Marry when June roses grow, over land and sea you'll go.
Those who in July do wed, must labor for their daily bread.
Whoever wed in August be, many a change is sure to see.
Marry in September's shrine, your living will be rich and fine.
If in October you do marry, love will come but riches tarry.
If you wed in bleak November, only joys will come, remember.
When December snows fall fast, marry and true love will last.

Wedding Facts

The longest wedding dress train measured 3,949.8 feet and was made by Cindy Predhomme and France Loridan in Caudry, France on August 5, 2006.

Previously, British glamour model Jordan, aka Katie Price, had held the record. She walked down the aisle to wed singer Peter Andre on September 10, 2005, in a dress measuring some 2,700 feet.

Lauren and David Blair of Tennessee hold the world record for the most marriage-vows renewals of any one couple. They exchanged vows for the eighty-third time on August 16, 2004, at the Boardwalk Hotel and Casino in Las Vegas, having first married in 1984.

Suresh Joachim, who wed in Ontario, Canada in 2003, holds the record for the most bridesmaids at a wedding. She had

♥♥♥♥♥♥♥♥♥♥♥♥♥♥♥♥♥♥♥♥♥♥♥♥♥♥♥♥♥♥♥♥♥♥♥

seventy-nine attendants on her special day – it's a miracle any-one else was able to get inside the venue.

TYING THE KNOT

The phrase 'to tie the knot' – meaning 'to marry' – has many possible origins. The earliest suggestion comes from the Roman era, when the bride would wear a girdle that was tied into knots; some say the expression stems from this custom. (The groom, of course, could later enjoy unpicking each intricate tangle.)

Perhaps the most commonly proposed source is that of pagan handfasting ceremonies (which in fact remained legal wedding services in Scotland until 1939). The term 'handfasting' originates in the Anglo-Saxon word 'handfœstung', which means the shaking of hands to seal a contract. In this traditional rite, the couple's clasped hands are tied together by a cord or ribbon, symbolizing their eternal unity.

The tradition isn't just European. In Africa, some countries practise a tradition whereby braided grasses bind the hands of the newlyweds to represent their new alliance, while during an Indian Vedic wedding, the bride's hand is loosely tied to her husband's. In a Northern Thai Buddhist ceremony, the couple are bound both by the wrists and by the head, to symbolize the union of mind and body.

The oldest bride ever to get married was 102-year-old Minnie Munro from Australia, who wed eighty-three-year-old Dudley Reid in May 1991.

The oldest groom is Harry Stevens, who at the grand old age of 103 married eighty-four-year-old Thelma Lucas at the Caravilla Retirement Home in Beloit, Wisconsin in December 1984.

GRETNA GREEN

This small Scottish town is famous across the globe as a wedding venue. After England passed the 1754 Marriage Act, which demanded parental consent for marriages if either party was under twenty-one, the only possible destination for determined young lovebirds was nearby Scotland. Gretna Green was conveniently located just over the border, and allowed anyone over sixteen to wed, no further questions asked.

Though marriage laws are more liberal in this day and age, the town still attracts those brides and grooms, hosting 5,000 weddings a year.

The Big Day: Unique Unions

Not all weddings are white . . .

In November 2005, Dai Edwards didn't let his fear of heights get in the way of his marrying fiancée Jackie Young in a 72-foot-tall lighthouse. The first couple in Britain to wed in such a building tied the knot at the top of Smeaton's Tower on Plymouth Hoe.

Embarking on a rather extreme version of kiss chase, in 1999 Croydon couple Mick Gambrill and Barbara Cole married midway through the London Marathon, stopping off for a Greenwich ceremony in their custom-made outfits, before later finishing the race.

It was 'bottoms up!' in a brewery for newlyweds Richard and Karen Burr: in October 2007 they became the first couple to tie the knot at Shepherd Neame's brewery in Faversham, Kent. Hops were used for decorations.

When Horatio Nelson was asked if he considered the day of the Nile victory (the Battle of the Nile, August 1, 1798) the happiest of his life, he replied: 'No; the happiest was that on which I married Lady Nelson.'

Jo and Tony Cox planned a 1940s-style wedding in honour of the fact that they'd met at a 1940s vintage dance. A blackout signalled the bride's arrival, while recordings of bombs falling and Chamberlain's speech declaring war provided the soundtrack. All the guests dressed up in period costume, then jitterbugged to their heart's content at the reception.

♥♥♥♥♥♥♥♥♥♥♥♥♥♥♥♥♥♥♥♥♥♥♥♥♥♥♥♥♥♥♥♥♥♥♥♥

♥▼♥▼♥▼♥▼♥▼♥▼♥▼♥▼♥▼♥▼♥▼♥▼♥▼♥▼♥▼♥▼♥▼♥

The score was love-love when Mike and Debbie Evetts got hitched at a ping-pong-themed wedding in 2007. They exited the ceremony under an arch of bats, and the groom happily squeezed in five sets before the first dance.

CHAPEL OF LOVE

The infamous Little Church of the West in Las Vegas has been the venue for countless celebrity weddings. Here are just a handful of the famous couples who have exchanged their vows at the popular chapel in the Nevada desert.

Bob Geldof and Paula Yates (June 1986)

Dudley Moore and Brogan Lane (February 1988)

Richard Gere and Cindy Crawford (December 1991)

Noel Gallagher and Meg Mathews (June 1997)

Chris Evans and Billie Piper (May 2001)

Unfortunately, marrying at such a venue doesn't guarantee lifelong happiness together, as each of the above couples later divorced . . .

Daredevil Richard Baldwin discounted the idea of arriving at his wedding ceremony in a car, on horseback or by motorbike. Even a helicopter wasn't quite dramatic enough. Instead, he skydived to the venue from 6,000 feet. His bride was probably expecting it – having been proposed to at 5,000 feet on a tandem parachute jump. That's one way to sweep a girl off her feet . . .

♥▼♥▼♥▼♥▼♥▼♥▼♥▼♥▼♥▼♥▼♥▼♥▼♥▼♥▼♥▼♥▼♥▼♥

'A love song is just a caress set to music.'
SIGMUND ROMBERG

The First Dance

In a 2007 survey by the Wedding TV channel, the following songs were voted as the most popular tunes to which newly-weds danced their first dance.

1 'I Will Always Love You' by Whitney Houston

2 'Endless Love' by Lionel Richie and Diana Ross

3 'Angels' by Robbie Williams

= 3 'Wonderful Tonight' by Eric Clapton

5 'I Don't Want to Miss a Thing' by Aerosmith

6 'Unchained Melody' by The Righteous Brothers

7 'We've Only Just Begun' by The Carpenters

8 'When a Man Loves a Woman' by Percy Sledge

9 'From This Moment' by Shania Twain and Bryan White

10 'Truly Madly Deeply' by Savage Garden

'Love is like a violin. The music may stop now and then, but the strings remain forever.'
ANONYMOUS

♥♥

SONG FACTS

In 2004, Yoko Ono had a number-one hit on the US dance chart with a revamped version of her 1984 song 'Every Man Has a Woman Who Loves Him', entitled 'Every Man Has a Man Who Loves Him', in support of gay marriage. She also recorded a lesbian interpretation of the same track.

The most popular word to appear in a hit song is 'love'.

'If music be the food of love, play on.'
Twelfth Night, Act I, Scene i,
WILLIAM SHAKESPEARE

Your Song

Many couples have a melody that is 'theirs': a song that summons all their emotions and represents for both lovers exactly how they feel about one another.

Make the most of such a powerful amulet. Play it on the important occasions – as well as at those times when you want to share a special moment with your lover. Dance to it, and sing to it, and love through it. Consider writing out the lyrics in beautiful calligraphy, then framing the artwork and giving it as a gift to your soulmate.

♥♥

Love in the Animal Kingdom

L IKE humans, animals often grow attached to a partner, building a bond together that lasts for years (lifespan permitting, of course). Here are some animals that find their soulmates and stick to them like glue – quite literally, in one rather horrid case . . .

Lovebirds

Perhaps predictably, many species of lovebirds pair for life. These famous, brightly colored birds take their romantic name from the way in which mating couples affectionately groom each other, and from their desire to remain in close proximity to their loved one. In French, they are known as *les inséparables*.

Whooping Cranes

Following complex mating dances and calls – which include head tosses, jumps, bows, wing flutters and the chucking about of flimsy items such as grass and feathers – these endangered birds mate for life, sometimes staying together for ten or fifteen years. They raise only one chick a year and are the tallest birds in North America: you could say love makes everyone stand that little bit straighter.

♥♥

♥ ♥

Swans

Perhaps the most famous of all the creatures that mate for life, these majestic waterbirds have become an enduring symbol of love. Touchingly, when two swans swim close together, the joint curve of their S-shaped necks forms the contours of a heart.

Anglerfish

These scary-looking creatures have a similarly scary-sounding mating process. When the male locates a female, he jumps on board with a quick nibble of her flank, releasing an enzyme that fuses their bodies together (these two really do mate for life; divorce doesn't exist in the world of the anglerfish).

After their union, the male becomes entirely dependent on the female for food and protection, and quickly degenerates, losing his eyes and all internal organs. Essentially he becomes an in-house sperm bank for the female whenever she wants to reproduce, and remains parasitically attached to her forever.

Titi Monkeys

Titi monkeys are affectionate primates who regularly hold hands, link tails, nuzzle and sit close together in their mating pairs. Somewhat unusually in the animal kingdom, couples seem to place their intimacy above all else. Indeed, research

♥ ♥

psychologists Sally P. Mendoza and William A. Mason observed that parents were sometimes more attached to one another than to any of their offspring. Like humans, titi monkeys become distressed and sad when separated from their other halves.

THE WEB OF LOVE

Spare a thought for the poor spider amidst this celebration of lifelong partnerships. Famously, some male spiders have become the female's lunch after they have mated, but often this is simply because the female is hungry – a dire case of the post-coital munchies – or she mistook the male for prey.

Clever males attempt to get round this by bringing such gifts as a tasty fly for their chosen one, or performing elaborate mating rituals so that the female realizes their intention. As a result, it's fairly rare for a male to be eaten by his mate: the exception (there's always one) is the redback spider, which eats its mate 60 percent of the time.

Doves

Another enduring symbol of love, doves abide by the vow 'till death do us part', remaining in their mating couples for life and sharing the responsibility of raising a family. In Greek and Roman mythology, the dove was the sacred bird of the goddess of love, Aphrodite/Venus.

♥ ♥

Animal Love Facts

* In 2007, scientists began playing romantic music to sharks at ten Sea Life Centers in Germany. The aim was to put the big fish in the mood for love, as reproduction rates had dropped sharply.

* Approximately 3 percent of pet owners give their animal a gift on Valentine's Day.

* Anthropologists have found that animals display 'kissing' behavior as a sign of affection, naming dogs, moles, turtles and dolphins as species most likely to pucker up.

* Star and Syd, a couple of boxer dogs, 'wed' in September 2002 in Clifton, England in aid of Bristol dogs' shelter – and true love, of course. Owner Annie Tombs said before the ceremony: 'They're inseparable. They adore each other . . . Instead of exchanging rings, they plan to exchange collars.'

* A vicar from Brockworth, England, found himself in the spotlight when he blessed two dogs in what was misconstrued by the local media as a mock marriage ceremony. Labrador Saul got 'hitched' to crossbreed Foxy in August 2004.

* After his mate Rexanne was tragically eaten by a fox, Rex the widowed swan turned to the Internet to mend his broken heart. In 2007, staff at his home, the Trevano Garden, set up the Facebook group Rex the Black-Necked Swan is Looking For Love.

♥ ♥

Kiss Me Quick

'I married the first man I ever kissed. When I tell this to my children, they just about throw up.'

BARBARA BUSH

KISSING is one of the best things about being in love. Nothing is nicer than a lovely long smooch with your beloved. There are endless kisses and quick kisses, wet kisses and dry kisses, passionate kisses and perfunctory pecks, Eskimo and butterfly and all sorts of other kisses.

Even the word – 'kiss', with its insistent 'k', drawn-out 'i' and sexy, sibilant 'ss' – summons up the sensuality of the moment when your loved one's lips meet yours. The scientific term for kissing – 'osculation', from the Latin verb *osculari* – doesn't work quite so well . . .

It Started With a Kiss

The origins of kissing are somewhat mysterious. Professor Vaughn M. Bryant of Texas A&M University found that the earliest reference to kissing came in some Vedic texts that dated back to 1500 B.C.

Many anthropologists believe that the practice evolved from sniffing each other, theorizing that the act of pressing our lips together was the next obvious step after rubbing noses.

♥♥♥♥♥♥♥♥♥♥♥♥♥♥♥♥♥♥♥♥♥♥♥♥♥♥♥♥♥♥♥♥♥♥♥♥♥

The Tinguian people of the Philippines don't actually lock lips to kiss. Instead, they put their lips close to their partner's – and inhale.

Pucker Up: A Collection of Kissing Trivia

In Roman times, husbands would embrace their wives when they came home from work, and plant a smacker on their lips. But it wasn't a sign that they'd missed their lovers, or an ancient version of 'Hi, honey, I'm home!' Instead, they were checking whether or not their wives had been at the bottle during the day, testing for the telltale taste of alcohol!

A kiss has been symbolized by the letter 'x' since at least 1763.

The first screen kiss was between John Rice and May Irwin in the aptly named *The Kiss* (1896). It was a short film lasting only twenty seconds, and showed the closing moment of the Broadway play *The Widow Jones*. The movie caused outrage at the time.

According to records website www.thelongestlistofthelongeststuffatthelongestdomainnameatlonglast.com, the longest kiss

♥♥♥♥♥♥♥♥♥♥♥♥♥♥♥♥♥♥♥♥♥♥♥♥♥♥♥♥♥♥♥♥♥♥♥♥♥

of all time was between twenty-six-year-old James Belshaw and twenty-three-year-old Sophia Severin.

On July 11, 2005, they locked lips for an astonishing thirty-one hours, thirty minutes and thirty seconds. That's a seriously spun-out smooch.

In 2006, an Israeli couple were prosecuted under India's obscenity laws for kissing at their Hindu wedding ceremony in Pushkar, Rajasthan.

Kissing also has an important role to play in children's fairy tales. Sleeping Beauty is awakened by a kiss, while the Frog Prince is transformed from reptile to handsome dish by a loving peck on his mouth.

In September 2007, nearly 7,000 couples kissed for ten seconds in Tuzla, Bosnia to try to set a new world record. That's a whole lotta loving.

It's estimated over 5 million bacteria are exchanged between lovers during a single kiss. That makes brushing your teeth beforehand seem something of a triviality.

♥ ▼ ♥ ▼ ♥ ▼ ♥ ▼ ♥ ▼ ♥ ▼ ♥ ▼ ♥ ▼ ♥ ▼ ♥ ▼ ♥ ▼ ♥ ▼ ♥ ▼ ♥ ▼ ♥ ▼ ♥ ▼ ♥ ▼ ♥

Types of Kiss

Eskimo

This is the act of rubbing noses with your lover. It's an urban myth that this practice evolved among the Inuit people due to the cold weather in their part of the world (Inuit couples who kissed on the lips supposedly ran the risk of becoming stuck together). Instead, the practice harks back to the sensuous act of inhaling your partner's scent.

Butterfly

The delicate practice of batting your eyelashes against your partner's skin.

THE ART OF KISSING

The sculptor Auguste Rodin created a piece in marble entitled *The Kiss*. It was originally called *Francesca da Rimini* and depicted her forbidden love for her husband's brother, Paolo Malatesta, as described in Dante's *Inferno*. Some find the raw passion of the sculpture unsettling – as late as 1997, it was barred from a traveling exhibit of Rodin's work.

The artists Edvard Munch, Gustav Klimt and Francesco Hayez have all painted pictures entitled *The Kiss*. Klimt's is perhaps the most famous – it is currently exhibited in the Österreichisches Galerie in Vienna, and would be well worth a visit if you and your lover ever take a trip to the romantic Austrian city.

♥♥♥♥♥♥♥♥♥♥♥♥♥♥♥♥♥♥♥♥♥♥♥♥♥♥♥♥♥♥♥♥♥♥♥♥♥

> 'The Eskimos had fifty-two names for snow
> because it was important to them: there ought to be
> as many for love.'
> **MARGARET ATWOOD**

Caterpillar

Rubbing eyebrows with your lover. No, I'm not sure why you'd do this, either.

Vacuum

The 1936 manual *The Art of Kissing* recommends this specialized 'suction' kiss, saying that 'a delicious sense of torpor will creep over your entire body, giving a lassitude that is almost beatific.' It describes the required action as similar to that used 'to draw out the innards of an orange'. Nice.

French

A kiss using tongues. This kiss has the most number of slang words attributed to it worldwide: in Bosnia they call it '?*vaka*' ('bubblegum'); the English population in Mauritius refer to it as 'grabbing'; in Slovenia, teenagers use the verb '*zalizati*' ('to

♥♥♥♥♥♥♥♥♥♥♥♥♥♥♥♥♥♥♥♥♥♥♥♥♥♥♥♥♥♥♥♥♥♥♥♥♥

lick someone'); Scots have been known to call it 'biting their face off'; while in Chile, the relevant verb is *comer*, 'to eat'.

Confusingly, in southern India, the term 'English kiss' is used.

THE MAGIC OF MISTLETOE

One of the big benefits of the winter season is the prevalence of mistletoe: tradition dictates that a couple standing beneath a sprig of this festive plant should kiss.

Mistletoe has long connections with love and fertility, and the kissing tradition may have evolved from an ancient fertility rite.

Every time a kiss takes place under a branch of mistletoe, a berry should be plucked from it. When all the berries are gone, it becomes bad luck to kiss beneath the plant.

Somewhat unromantically, the Anglo-Saxon-derived name translates as 'dung on a twig'.

Memory Lane

Part of the joy of long-term loving is the wealth of memories you accrue together. Whether it was a perfect day, the first time you kissed, or even an awful holiday that you can now look back on and laugh about, that shared history is something quite special. So it makes perfect sense to revisit the memories every now and again.

A Holiday Romance

Vacations often provide the most va-va-voom memories – be it because of the bliss of being together 24/7, the picturesque surroundings, the freedom from everyday pressures or simply the sun going to your heads. Why not re-create those recollections once in a while? Whether for a special occasion or 'just because', you and your partner are guaranteed an evening of intimate nostalgia.

Not sure where to start? Here are a couple of tasty recipes (together with a few tips) to help you stage either an Italian or Grecian trip down memory lane.

If you've never been to either of those countries, the recipes and tips work just as well as a pre-holiday taster, or for an unrelated cozy night in.

> 'A lady of forty-seven who has been married twenty-seven years and has six children knows what love really is and once described it for me like this: "Love is what you've been through with somebody."'
>
> **JAMES THURBER**

Setting the Scene

As with all thoughtful surprises for lovers, the most successful are those planned with their personal preferences in mind. Remember, too, that this is an evening that aims to reproduce the glory of your holiday. If the two of you enjoyed a cheap and cheerful break in a very touristy spot, don't be tempted to upgrade on your return home.

Similarly, if your time away was the epitome of chic cosmopolitan travel, then decorating your dining room with flags and incorporating said flag's colors into the design of the table placements is perhaps not the classiest way to re-create those romantic evenings out.

Here are some further suggestions of how to make the night more memorable:

* Music, Maestro! For the perfect romantic setting, why not opt for your holiday destination's traditional music? The theme from *Zorba the Greek* is internationally renowned; or Verdi's *La Traviata* could work wonders (as it did for Julia Roberts's character in *Pretty Woman*).

* Dress for the occasion. In the midst of winter, why not wear your favorite summer outfit? You'll be indoors, so

you won't catch cold. Seeing your loved one in out-of-season attire will summon up instant fond memories of shared times past.

TIP!
Consider matching your background music to that played in your favorite restaurant on holiday.

✴ Alternatively, why not sit outside, whatever the weather? Wrap up warm, place thick blankets over your lover's knees, and then enjoy the fresh breeze and the cool night air as you would on holiday.

✴ A candlelit table is a must. Can you find candle holders to match those in the restaurant? Or would the bohemian candle-in-a-wine-bottle approach be best?

✴ Think about the aperitif. Perhaps you could learn to mix your partner's favored pre-dinner cocktail.

✴ If there was a wine you particularly enjoyed together, why not purchase a couple of bottles while you're in the region, to be relished at home over the next few months? Tonight would be just the night to luxuriate in a bottle or two.

'There is nothing like an odor to stir memories.'
WILLIAM MCFEE

---

vv

CUSTOMIZED CUISINE

The recipes included here are simply suggestions. Which dishes did you and your partner savor during your time away? You may find them more suited to your plans.

If you can't find a recipe for the dishes in your own cookbooks, excellent recipe websites now abound, so you're likely to be able to track down instructions and ingredients lists via the Internet. Or you could ask the waiter for the recipe of your favorite dish on your last night away.

Idyllic Italy

Italian food is one of the most popular cuisines in the world, so it's no wonder that its source country is one of the most well-visited tourist destinations. Eatables aside, Italy is also a nation of great passion – home to romantic artists such as Botticelli and da Vinci; the adopted abode of writers like Shelley, Byron and the Brownings; the setting of some of Shakespeare's most famous plays (including *Romeo and Juliet*); the origin of operas by Puccini . . .

Whether you and your lover navigated the canals of Venice, meandered the streets of Rome, or sampled the sensational coast of the Adriatic Sea, your treasured memories can be re-created in the comfort of your own home.

The Starter:
Tomato, Basil and Mozzarella Salad

Serves two
You will need:
1 large ball buffalo mozzarella
1 pint cherry tomatoes
(roughly 250 g or 9 oz)
8 leaves fresh basil
drizzle of olive oil
ground pepper to season

Tip!

Don't skimp on the quality of your ingredients.
This starter is out of this world when prepared with
the finest, freshest fare, but will be decidedly
underwhelming with economy cheese and
just-on-the-turn tomatoes.

Method:

1. Cut the mozzarella into even, ½-inch-thick slices. Divide equally between two plates.

2. Halve the cherry tomatoes, then add to the plate of mozzarella. You can create patterns if desired – hearts, smiley faces – or simply arrange elegantly next to the cheese.

3. Take the basil leaves and arrange four on each plate.

4. Drizzle a tiny amount of olive oil very lightly over the salad, and add ground black pepper to taste. Serve immediately.

♥ ♥

The Main Course:
Tomato and Goats' Cheese Lasagne

SERVES FOUR
You will need:
2.2 lb assorted fresh tomatoes
1 tbsp olive oil
3 tsp granulated sugar
2 tsp dried oregano
9 oz closed cup mushrooms
10.5 oz goats' cheese
1 jar fresh green pesto
(approximately 5.5 oz)
4 fresh lasagne sheets
1 oz Parmesan cheese
black pepper to season

Method:

1. Preheat the oven to 400°F.

2. Chop all the tomatoes. Put a quarter of these to one side. Cook the remainder with some olive oil in a covered saucepan, over a medium heat for 5 minutes, stirring very occasionally. Add the sugar and oregano, and then remove from the heat.

3. Next, quarter the mushrooms. Place in a covered bowl in the microwave. Cook for 4 minutes on full power.

4. Spoon the cooked mushrooms into the pan containing the cooked tomatoes, discarding any excess cooking juices.

5. In a separate bowl, combine the goats' cheese and pesto.

6. Layer the ingredients in an oblong casserole dish approximately 10 × 13 inches. First layer the tomato/mushroom mixture (including the cooking juices from the

♥♥♥♥♥♥♥♥♥♥♥♥♥♥♥♥♥♥♥♥♥♥♥♥♥♥♥♥♥♥♥♥♥♥♥♥♥♥♥

tomatoes), then add a layer of fresh pasta spread with the cheese/pesto sauce. Place the lasagne sheet cheese-side down in the dish. Add another layer of the tomato/mushroom mix then follow with another sheet of cheese-coated lasagne, again placed cheese-side down.

TIP!

Try cutting the cheese into small pieces before you stir together the cheese and the pesto.

---

7. Repeat the layers until all the ingredients have been used and the dish is full, ensuring you finish with a layer of lasagne.

8. Top with the uncooked tomatoes and season.

9. Cover the dish and bake in the oven for 30 minutes.

10. Top with the Parmesan and bake for a further 5 to 10 minutes, until the cheese has melted and is bubbling.

11. Serve with a leafy green salad or green beans.

Gorgeous Greece

Greece and her islands are renowned for their good weather, beautiful environments and captivating mythology. It's no wonder that this location is enduringly popular for romantically inclined travellers. Of course, it's up to the pair of you whether or not you decide to play Musical Grecian Statues after dinner . . .

♥♥♥♥♥♥♥♥♥♥♥♥♥♥♥♥♥♥♥♥♥♥♥♥♥♥♥♥♥♥♥♥♥♥♥♥♥♥♥

♥♥

The Starter: Baked Feta

SERVES TWO
You will need:
7 oz feta cheese
2 tomatoes
half a small red onion
1 or 2 cloves garlic, according to taste
1 tsp grated lemon zest
3 leaves fresh oregano, chopped
drizzle of olive oil
pinch of salt and pepper

Method:

1. Preheat the oven to 350°F. Cut out a piece of aluminum foil 12 inches in length.

2. Cut the block of feta in half lengthwise and place one half in the middle of the tinfoil.

3. Slice the tomatoes, chop the onion and crush the garlic. Mix these prepared ingredients together in a bowl, adding the lemon zest and oregano.

4. Sprinkle half the mixture on top of the cheese in the tinfoil. Drizzle with a dash of olive oil.

5. Add the second half of the feta on top of the first.

6. Layer the remaining vegetable mixture on top, and drizzle with olive oil again. Season.

7. Close up the square of tinfoil to make a scrunched-up parcel.

8. Bake for 20 minutes, and be careful when opening the tinfoil as a lot of steam will escape.

9. Serve with crusty bread, or a small dish of olives.

♥♥

♥♥♥♥♥♥♥♥♥♥♥♥♥♥♥♥♥♥♥♥♥♥♥♥♥♥♥♥♥♥♥♥♥♥

'Your words are my food, your breath my wine.
You are everything to me.'

SARAH BERNHARDT

The Main Course:
Moussaka

SERVES FOUR
You will need:
1 onion
1 clove garlic (optional)
2 tbsp olive oil
1 lb minced lamb
1 14 oz can tomatoes
1 tbsp tomato purée
1 tsp dried herbs – mixed, or marjoram
salt and pepper
1 eggplant, cut into slices about
¼ inches thick
3.5 oz grated cheese
(Parmesan or strong cheddar)
2 eggs
½ cup cream

Method:

1 Preheat the oven to 350°F.

2 Fry the onion and garlic in a teaspoon of oil until the onion
softens and becomes transparent. Add the minced lamb

♥♥♥♥♥♥♥♥♥♥♥♥♥♥♥♥♥♥♥♥♥♥♥♥♥♥♥♥♥♥♥♥♥♥

and fry on a high heat, stirring well so that it browns quickly without sticking.

3 Add the tomatoes, tomato purée and herbs, then season to taste. Bring to simmering point and leave to cook for 30 minutes, either on the stovetop or in an ovenproof dish in the oven.

4 Meanwhile, prepare the eggplant. Either fry the slices in the rest of the oil (cooking them in a couple of batches) or place in the microwave with the oil, covered, and heat on full power for 5 minutes.

5 When the lamb is cooked, use a teaspoon to spoon off any fat that floats on the surface. If you have time to leave it to cool down, any fat will set and become even easier to remove. Check the seasoning of the mince is as you desire.

6 Layer the eggplant and lamb in an ovenproof dish approximately 6.75 inches in diameter, ending with a layer of eggplant. Sprinkle the cheese on top.

7 Beat together the eggs and cream, and season well. Gently pour the egg mixture over the dish.

8 Bake in the oven for 15 to 20 minutes, until the sauce is set and golden brown.

9 Serve with warm bread – a French baguette, pitas or a ciabatta – and a green salad.

TIP!

Cook the dish for 30 minutes if the meat is cold when the moussaka is assembled.

One Moment in Time

There's another great way to preserve special memories of your relationship. Why not spend an afternoon creating a time capsule of your love affair – to be opened at some distant point in the future? On your silver wedding anniversary, say, or when you both turn sixty.

Use a watertight container to hold your time-capsule items, and clearly label what the box is. Most importantly, don't forget where you stash it – up in the attic or in a writing table, perhaps, or buried under your favorite tree in the garden (as long as you're not planning to move house anytime soon).

It's definitely best to store it out of sight; that way, the contents will be forgotten more quickly, and your delight on rediscovering them will prove that much greater.

Time-Capsule Contents

You could include some of the following in your personalized time capsule:

* a recent photograph of you both
* a letter written by each of you to the other, not to be read until the time capsule is opened again
* a diary of the past year, which lists all the day-to-day events you've shared
* a written list of your favorite things: places, books, films, friends, etc.
* a summary of your joint ambitions for the future
* recent drawings by your young children, if you have kids
* a photograph of the house you're currently living in

❤❤❤❤❤❤❤❤❤❤❤❤❤❤❤❤❤❤❤❤❤❤❤❤❤❤❤❤❤❤❤❤❤❤❤❤❤

✳ detailed written descriptions of your favorite memories of time spent together (will the memories be as sharp when you read the descriptions in the years to come?)

✳ a CD recording of your favorite romantic songs

SNAP HAPPY

In this digital age, we all have photographs of our halcyon holidays, which recorded the special moments as they happened. But how often do you actually look at those pictures once you've picked them up from the shop, or loaded them on to your computer?

Don't let the snaps sit forgotten in a cupboard, the prints still in their plastic sleeve or the files stored on a soulless memory card. Make a point of making something of these visual treasures. As soon as you get back from your holiday, spend an afternoon looking at the snaps together, placing the best ones in a photograph album. Adding your own humorous captions is optional. At a later date, you can then easily take a wander down memory lane together, snuggled up on the sofa with this neat presentation of your vacation pictures.

This doesn't just apply to holiday snaps, of course – try to create a beautiful album to commemorate that day out, wedding, birthday surprise or mini-break. Frame the nicest pics and display them in your home.

❤❤❤❤❤❤❤❤❤❤❤❤❤❤❤❤❤❤❤❤❤❤❤❤❤❤❤❤❤❤❤❤❤❤❤❤

Love Laughs

A 'GSOH' – good sense of humour – is the number-one desirable attribute in lovers, as magazine surveys and ads in lonely-hearts columns frequently show. Here's a selection of love-based jokes, with which you can tickle your partner's funny bone.

Q: Who did the vampire fall in love with?
A: The girl necks door.

Q: Why did the fish cross the road?
A: To be with his sole mate.

Q: Why did the newlyweds walk into the wall?
A: Because love is blind.

A man, in a panic, runs into a doctor's surgery closely followed by his wife.

'Doctor, doctor,' he says, 'I think I'm turning into a door.'

'No, darling,' says his wife, patiently. 'I said, "You're adored."'

Q: Why did the comedian refuse to tell jokes about romance?
A: Because he didn't find love a laughing matter.

▼▼▼▼▼▼▼▼▼▼▼▼▼▼▼▼▼▼▼▼▼▼▼▼▼▼▼▼▼▼▼▼▼▼▼▼▼▼

Q: What do you get if you cross a chicken with Casanova?
A: An egg-ceptional lover.

The joke website www.lifeisajoke.com polled a group of primary-school children to discover their thoughts on love and marriage. The results are hilarious.

What is the right age to get married?
Twenty-three is the best age because you know the person forever by then.

CAMILLE, age ten

What do most people do on a date?
On the first date, they just tell each other lies, and that usually gets them interested enough to go for a second date.

MARTIN, age ten

When is it okay to kiss someone?
The rule goes like this: if you kiss someone, then you should marry them and have kids with them. It's definitely the right thing to do.

HOWARD, age eight

How would you make a marriage work?
Tell your wife that she looks pretty even if she looks like a ten-ton truck.

RICKY, age ten

'In those whom I like, I can find no common denominator; in those whom I love, I can: they all make me laugh.'

W. H. AUDEN

▼▼▼▼▼▼▼▼▼▼▼▼▼▼▼▼▼▼▼▼▼▼▼▼▼▼▼▼▼▼▼▼▼▼▼▼▼▼

Love Letters

THERE is something very special about a love letter. Perhaps
it is simply seeing affection written out in black and white:
it communicates feelings much more solidly than formless
sweet nothings whispered in an ear, or terms of endearment
traced lovingly on tender skin.

Love letters are a very traditional form of expressing emotion,
an art that is sadly no longer much practised in this digital age
of text messaging and e-mail. But in the past, love letters were
often the only way that lovers could communicate.

Héloise and Abelard

These twelfth-century Parisian lovers came together when
Peter Abelard, a churchman, was hired by Héloise's uncle to be
her tutor. Despite his commitment to the church, Abelard
could not help but fall in love with Héloise, a beautiful and
well-educated young woman, and so they secretly married.

When Héloise's uncle discovered their passion for one another, he was furious. Abelard sent Héloise to a convent for her own protection. But the uncle, thinking that Abelard intended to renounce his niece, had Abelard castrated. Forced apart, and with few options, Héloise became a nun and Abelard a monk. However, they continued to write to each other and express their enduring love, despite their separation, for the rest of their lives.

The following extract comes from one of Héloise's many love letters to Abelard:

> You know, beloved, as the whole world knows, how much I have lost in you, how at one wretched stroke of fortune that supreme act of flagrant treachery robbed me of my very self in robbing me of you . . . You alone have the power to make me sad, to bring me happiness or comfort . . . God knows I never sought anything in you except yourself; I wanted simply you.

Edited and translated by B. Radice, *Epistola* (1974)

'Love vanquishes time. To lovers, a moment can be eternity, eternity can be the tick of a clock.'
MARY PARRISH

Napoléon and Josephine

The future Emperor and Empress of France first met in 1795 and were wed less than a year later on March 9, 1796. Due to Napoléon's military commitments, they were often separated for long periods. The letters of the lonely Bonaparte to his distant wife are famous to this day.

Despite a number of infidelities on both sides, by the time of their 1805 coronation they were fully committed to one other. They divorced in 1810 only because Josephine was unable to produce an heir. At the divorce ceremony, each read out a statement of devotion to the other.

Following Josephine's 1814 death, upon Napoléon's return to France after exile, he went to her garden and collected violets, her favorite flower. He kept the blooms in a locket that he wore daily, as a constant reminder of their passion, until his own death in 1821.

Here is an extract of a letter from Napoléon to Josephine, written in Marmirolo, Italy on July 17, 1796:

> Incessantly I live over in my memory your caresses, your tears, your affectionate solicitude. The charms of the incomparable Josephine kindle continually a burning and a glowing flame in my heart . . . I thought that I loved you months ago, but since my separation from you I feel that I love you a thousandfold more . . . Believe me, it is not in my power to have a single thought which is not of thee.

Elizabeth Barrett Browning and Robert Browning

In 1844, Elizabeth Barrett was a thirty-nine-year-old spinster, confined to singledom by her father's eccentric dictate that none of his children should marry, and virtually housebound by various illnesses that incapacitated her. She was also the author of a well-received volume of poems.

On 10 January 1845, thirty-two-year-old Robert Browning, also a poet, wrote to Ms. Barrett to express his admiration for her work. It was the start of a correspondence that produced almost 600 letters over twenty months; the start of one of the most romantic courtships in history.

They finally met after five months, and many epistles. Browning is believed to have declared his affection for her immediately, but Elizabeth gave a measured response to his passion. By January 1846, however, his support and love for her were sweeping her *onto* her feet – up off her sickbed and, eventually, out into the world. She later credited him with saving her life.

In September 1846, Elizabeth defied her father and married Robert Browning in a secret ceremony. She was immediately disowned when her father found out. The poets moved to Italy, where they had a son, Robert, and spent the next fifteen years happily married and writing poetry.

Elizabeth died in her husband's arms on June 29, 1861.

The following extract is taken from a letter written by Robert Browning on October 23, 1845, two days after seeing Elizabeth:

> I love you because I *love* you; I see you 'once a week' because I cannot see you all day long; I think of you all day long because I most certainly could not think of you once an hour less, if I tried . . .

'Love is the irresistible desire to be irresistibly desired.'
MARK TWAIN

▼ ♥

GIFT IDEA

Looking for a romantic gift idea? Why not give your partner a volume of love letters from some of the most celebrated writers of our times? The heated correspondence between the Brownings, French writer Anaïs Nin and novelist Henry Miller, and writers F. Scott and Zelda Fitzgerald have all been published in individual volumes. And that's just a handful to get you started.

Parting is Such Sweet Sorrow

Love letters come into their own when lovers are apart. They may not have the immediacy of an ardent phone conversation, or the convenience of e-mail, but who ever wanted romance to be 'convenient', anyway? What letters say, better than either of these media, is 'I'm thinking of you.'

The decreasing popularity of 'snail mail', too, means that the missives are almost always a welcome surprise.

Messages From Miles Away

If you're going away without your partner – be it for a business trip, a holiday with friends, or a recurring return to a long-distance home far away – why not send your partner a series of letters, cards or notes in the post to ease that transition from togetherness to separation?

Write your messages ahead of time. The day before you go, post one letter. It will arrive for your lover on the day of your

♥♥♥♥♥♥♥♥♥♥♥♥♥♥♥♥♥♥♥♥♥♥♥♥♥♥♥♥♥♥♥♥♥♥♥♥♥

departure. (This works best if you're leaving early in the morning, so they have a message from you as soon as they wake up, even though you're already on the road.)

Post another card from the airport or at some other stage of your journey. It'll give another boost to your partner's spirits in a day or so's time.

Finally, enlist the help of a friend to post a third letter the day after you leave. The best packages always come in threes.

> 'I am mad about you Dear Heart and sick at the thought of our parting and the days of separation and longing that are to follow . . . Perhaps when I am once more on land my mental vision may be clearer – at present, in the whole universe I see but one thing, am conscious of but one thing, you, and our love for each other.'
>
> **EDITH WHARTON** to her lover W. Morton Fullerton, c.20 May 1908, *The Letters of Edith Wharton* (eds. R. W. B. and Nancy Lewis)

When the Cat's Away . . .

If you're the partner left at home, don't be disheartened by your lover's absence. Write them a letter every day they're away, telling them how much you're missing them and what you've been up to – all that miscellanea you'd normally chat about each evening, but which you can't discuss while they're away.

Post your letters to them, either one day at a time, or in a pack at the end of the week. Date and time each of your letters – the one you wrote in your lunch hour at work; the one you

♥♥♥♥♥♥♥♥♥♥♥♥♥♥♥♥♥♥♥♥♥♥♥♥♥♥♥♥♥♥♥♥♥♥♥♥♥

♥♥♥♥♥♥♥♥♥♥♥♥♥♥♥♥♥♥♥♥♥♥♥♥♥♥♥♥♥♥♥♥♥♥♥♥♥♥♥

wrote after dinner with friends; the one you wrote at 3 a.m., when you just couldn't sleep without them next to you.

'To write a good love letter, you ought to begin without knowing what you mean to say, and to finish without knowing what you have written.'

JEAN JACQUES ROUSSEAU

Tips for Sending Love in the Mail

Handwritten letters are simply the best and will seem the most heartfelt, so don't be tempted to use a computer unless your writing is truly illegible.

To heighten the romance stakes, fill the envelope with rose petals, or squirt a *small* amount of your favorite scent on to the paper (do this before you write the letter, otherwise the cologne may smudge your words).

Write 'S.W.A.L.K.' on the back of the closed envelope – meaning 'Sealed With A Loving Kiss.'

Don't just mail notes. Why not hide them in your partner's favorite novel, to be discovered months or even years later when they return to the book, as you know they eventually will?

'And ever has it been that love knows not its own depth until the hour of separation.'

KAHLIL GIBRAN

♥♥♥♥♥♥♥♥♥♥♥♥♥♥♥♥♥♥♥♥♥♥♥♥♥♥♥♥♥♥♥♥♥♥♥♥♥♥♥

♥ ♥

Are there any other unexpected hiding places you could use? How about your lover's wallet, handbag or briefcase?

Why limit yourself to letters? Order CDs, flowers, wine and other treats for your partner, and don't breathe a word that they're on their way.

Postpone the moment. Write a love letter, but seal it. Instruct your partner to keep it safe and sealed, but to open it at some distant date in the future: perhaps a year and a day from the day you gave it to them, or in ten years' time, or on a special anniversary.

COOL COMMUNICATION

Ever thought about employing fridge magnets in your quest to communicate with your lover? Invest in a magnetic alphabet and go crazy. You can leave love notes for your partner about anything you want – a simple 'I love you', a request for a kiss, a thank-you message, a suggestive 'Dinner at eight in our fave place.'

Just make sure you don't end up using them for a tired old shopping list or demands to clean the bathroom: that would be missing the point entirely.

♥ ♥

The Perfect Gift

I T can sometimes be difficult to think of the ideal present for your partner, whether you're honoring an anniversary, their birthday, Christmas or other holidays – especially if you've been together for years.

The perfect gift will always be the one that is tailored to their individual desires and fancies. Remember: practical is not always perfect, even if they really do need a new hedge trimmer.

If you're utterly stuck, though, and inspiration refuses to strike, these gift suggestions may just turn out to be what your lover desperately wanted after all.

Top Ten Gift Suggestions

1 *Exhilarating experiences.*
Book your lover a rally-driving course, a hot-air balloon ride, white-water rafting, flying lessons or a sky-diving session.

Tip!

When a person undertakes a stimulating activity that involves perceived danger, such as riding a rollercoaster or driving a fast car, the chemicals released in the brain mirror those released when a person falls in love. So if you give your partner such an experience as a gift, it will re-create the heady chemical mix of the early days of your relationship.

❤ ❤

② *A posh night out planned to perfection.*
After drinks in a swanky bar and dinner in an even swankier restaurant, why not treat your lover to tickets at the ballet, opera or theatre? If they're more of a film buff, a viewing of an art-house flick should be appreciated. You could also hire a limo for the evening to really blow their socks off.

③ *Tickets to their favorite sporting event.*
Why not combine the main attraction with a mini-break in the nearest city?

④ *007 glamour.*
Every man wants to be just like James Bond, and every woman aspires to be a Bond girl. Plan a secret-service-themed evening, complete with full evening dress, fun gadget gifts, a rented sports car, shaken-not-stirred Martinis and a night out in a casino, perhaps in James's hometown, London.

⑤ *A romantic weekend away, just the two of you.*
Why not visit one of the magical mini-break destinations suggested on pages 76–81?

⑥ *A special piece of jewelry.*
You could have a new piece commissioned from a jewelry designer, or give the priceless gift of an old family heirloom.

⑦ *Tickets to their favorite live music gig.*
Whether it be a guitar band, a jazz trio, a classical concert, a pop star or a rock legend, your lover will be delighted to attend a performance of their favorite musical artist.

⑧ *A painting or other piece of art.*
Give them a gift with enduring pleasure, which is renewed whenever your partner gazes at the painting or sculpture.

❤ ❤

♥ ♥

⑨ A beer- or wine-based present.
Organize a brewery tour for the beer aficionado, with an additional gift package of various beers from around the world (and not just those brewed in your home country). For the vino enthusiast, a wine-tasting session with a case of their favorite tipple to take home afterwards should more than do the trick.

⑩ Give the gift of knowledge.
Why not book your lover a course of lessons in something they've always wanted to do, be it speaking Italian, ballroom dancing or playing the guitar?

TREASURE TRAIL

Add to the excitement of your partner's present by organizing a treasure hunt. Write out clues for them, each of which leads them to the next clue, until finally they arrive at their gift – which could be a wrapped package, or a destination itself. Alternatively, why not arrange an Easter-egg-style hunt, with gifts hidden around your home?

I'm Dreaming of December 25th

Christmas is a magical time of year full stop, but celebrating it with your lover adds an extra-special sparkle to the festive period. Make Christmas really romantic with some of the following ideas.

♥ ♥

♥♥

Treasured Traditions

One of the best elements of Christmas is the fact that it's steeped in tradition. Establish your own traditions with your lover to mark the season out as something just the two of you share.

Perhaps there's a favorite Christmas movie you'll watch every year, or a CD of festive tunes you like to listen to as you do the wrapping together. Maybe you'll plan an annual ice-skating trip in stunning surroundings, or make the Christmas shopping an adventure in an unknown location. Why not invent a seasonal dish that will always be on the menu in years to come?

Let it Snow

Is your lover a fan of white Christmases, yet the chance of snow in your area about as likely as the two of you ever splitting up? Take them to the snow instead – plan a trip to Lapland, or a skiing break in the Alps. Failing that, you could always hire a snow machine . . .

The Twelve Days of Christmas

While turtledoves and partridges in pear trees might not be your partner's ideal gifts, the premise behind this popular Christmas song is still a good one.

♥♥

Contrary to popular belief, the twelve days to which the song refers actually relate to the twelve days *after* Christmas – so you can surprise your beloved with even more gift-giving after the big day has passed.

Follow the song's suggestion of giving the number of items that relate to whether it's the first, second or twelfth day after Christmas, and so on (i.e. giving one, two or twelve specimens of a present). Gift ideas range from chocolate money to tangerines, from shoes to seedlings.

Santa, Baby

Let your lover relive childhood Christmas memories by preparing a stocking stuffed full of gifts for them. Hang it at the end of the bed, so that they'll see it as soon as they wake on Christmas morning.

Forget the Family

Lovely though your family are, spending Christmas with them can sometimes be a pressurized affair. Spend a least one Christmas Day in your life with your lover alone, and relish the intimate occasion. You can always catch up with the relatives the day after, after all.

♥♥♥♥♥♥♥♥♥♥♥♥♥♥♥♥♥♥♥♥♥♥♥♥♥♥♥♥♥♥♥♥♥♥♥♥♥♥♥

If it's impossible to make the actual day a treat for two, try to plan a moment or an evening at some point in the festive season that is solely for the pair of you to share.

Amorous Anniversaries

Lovers have a host of anniversaries they could celebrate each year: the first kiss, the first date, the official start of the relationship, the first holiday, moving in together, or possibly the wedding . . . Perhaps you've even gone so far as to commemorate a random date picked just for your lover: an annual day named in their honor, during which you spoil them rotten.

> 'Every anniversary . . . he gets a piece of construction paper. He folds it in half and puts "Tony loves Cherie". And there is a drawing of a little stick man and a little stick woman and loads of kisses.'
>
> **CHERIE BLAIR**

Whether you and your partner mark some, all or none of the above, chances are you honor at least one anniversary each year. Tradition holds that each wedding anniversary has a specific type of gift associated with it. Why not apply this guide to your own celebrations, married or not?

Listed on the next page are both the traditional gifts and more modern suggestions linked to particular anniversaries.

♥♥♥♥♥♥♥♥♥♥♥♥♥♥♥♥♥♥♥♥♥♥♥♥♥♥♥♥♥♥♥♥♥♥♥♥♥♥♥

137

♥♥♥

Anniversary	Traditional Gift	Modern Gift
First	Paper	Clocks
Second	Cotton/Straw	China
Third	Leather	Crystal/Glass
Fourth	Fruit/Flowers/Books	Electrical Appliances
Fifth	Wood	Silverware
Sixth	Sugar/Iron	Wood
Seventh	Wool/Copper	Desk Sets
Eighth	Bronze/Pottery	Linens/Lace
Ninth	Pottery/Willow	Leather
Tenth	Tin/Aluminum	Diamond Jewelry
Eleventh	Steel	Fashion Jewelry
Twelfth	Silk/Linen	Colored Gems/Pearls
Thirteenth	Lace	Textiles/Furs
Fourteenth	Ivory	Gold Jewelry
Fifteenth	Crystal	Watches
Twentieth	China	Bone China/Platinum
Twenty-Fifth	Silver	Silver
Thirtieth	Pearl	Diamond Jewelry
Thirty-Fifth	Coral	Jade
Fortieth	Ruby	Ruby
Forty-Fifth	Sapphire	Sapphire
Fiftieth	Gold	Gold
Fifty-Fifth	Emerald	Emerald
Sixtieth	Diamond	Diamond
Sixty-Fifth	Blue Sapphire	Star Sapphire
Seventieth	Diamond/Platinum	Platinum
Seventy-Fifth	Diamond	Diamond

♥♥♥

> 'Robert . . . began by keeping the anniversary of our marriage once a week.'
>
> **ELIZABETH BARRETT BROWNING**

Counting Down the Days

As anniversaries are always celebrated on a specific date, you could take advantage of this and add to your partner's anticipation by making them a personalized advent calendar that marks the passing time until your special day. Here's how.

You will need:
1 piece red construction paper
(or another color of your choice)
1 piece white construction paper
silver or gold marker pen
4 paper clips
craft knife
pencil
glue
items to hide behind the windows
(see suggestions on pages 142–3)
decorations as desired
(glitter, pressed flowers, etc.)

Method:

1 Decide how many days will be featured on your advent calendar.

♥ ♥

② Take the red piece of paper, which will be the top layer of the calendar. Leave a border of roughly 0.75 inches around the edge of the paper, and pencil a corresponding number of shapes for days on to it.

TIP!

These shapes will be the 'windows' in the calendar. Squares and rectangles are the easiest shapes to work with. Remember that the shapes will conceal your unique messages, so make them as large or small as you require.

---

③ Write a number on to each window using the marker pen, to signify the order in which the windows should be opened.

④ Place the paper on top of a firm surface that can be scratched, such as a chopping board. Use the craft knife to cut round three sides of the windows – traditionally, the top, bottom and right-hand side. Open up the windows.

⑤ Place the white paper beneath the red paper. Fix the two together using the paper clips. Using a pencil, mark out the shapes of the windows on the white paper.

⑥ Separate the pieces of paper. Close up the windows on the red paper, and place it to one side.

⑦ Fill the window shapes on the white paper with your personalized messages for your lover (see suggestions on pages 142 and 143). You may wish to rub out your original pencil marks afterwards.

♥ ♥

♥♥♥♥♥♥♥♥♥♥♥♥♥♥♥♥♥♥♥♥♥♥♥♥♥♥♥♥♥♥♥♥♥♥♥♥♥♥♥

Tip!

You could make the windows part of the decoration, *though you'll need to decide on this before you complete Step Two.* For example, you could lay out the windows in a heart shape, or spell out 'love' or your partner's name or initials.

Alternatively, you could draw your house, a romantic castle or your partner's face on the top layer of paper, with the windows marking actual windows and doors; turrets and ramparts; eyes, mouth and nose, respectively. You might even want to consider making the entire calendar heart-shaped.

8 Dab some glue around the edges of the white paper, and then glue the white and red papers together, with the red paper on top.

Tip!

Make sure your partner will easily be able to open the windows. If the windows are tightly closed, you could cut a tiny semi-circle halfway down each window's right-hand side, which will allow your partner to slide a finger beneath the top layer of paper. Alternatively, if the windows keep springing open, keep them in place with a small piece of Blu-Tack.

♥♥♥♥♥♥♥♥♥♥♥♥♥♥♥♥♥♥♥♥♥♥♥♥♥♥♥♥♥♥♥♥♥♥♥♥♥♥♥

▾▾▾

9 Decorate the red paper as desired. You could glue glitter to the edges, or over the top of the windows; stick pressed flowers in the corners; or illustrate the calendar with your own drawings.

Surprise!

Behind each window should be a personalized treat or message for your partner. Here are some suggestions of what you could include:

* ✱ a meaningful quote that reflects how you feel about your partner

* ✱ a self-penned short poem

* ✱ a promise to give your lover a long and lovely kiss, a foot massage, or a night off from the cooking

* ✱ a heart-shaped chocolate

* ✱ a photo of the two of you

* ✱ a romantic print or drawing

* ✱ a pressed flower

* ✱ a silver charm or small piece of jewelry

* ✱ a memory of something you've shared together – communicated through words or pictures

Perhaps the loveliest idea draws on some of the Christian advent calendars, which tell the story of Christmas in twenty-four 'chapters', one behind each window. Have a think about writing or illustrating a similar episodic tale for your lover. Ideas could include:

▾▾▾

* the story of your relationship, told sentence by sentence

* a tale about how you're going to treat your lover on the upcoming anniversary – each window could reveal a different treat

* a longer poem about your lover, recited one line at a time

* a description of how you feel about them

* an invented narrative, featuring your lover as the main character of your story

AN ADVENT CALENDAR IS FOR LIFE, NOT JUST FOR ANNIVERSARIES

An amorous advent calendar doesn't just succeed as an anniversary treat, of course. You could use one to tantalize your lover pre-proposal (they don't know what the days are counting down to . . . but you do), or pre-holiday, or before you take your lover out for a special evening.

Alternately, you could send your personalized calendar as a gift to a long-distance lover, so that they can mark the days before you'll see each other again.

Courtly Love

COURTLY love is an idealized form of love that was inspired, described and defined by the troubadour poetry of medieval times, originating in France. Very often it involved adultery, for this was an era in which marriages were made for political or financial gain and not for love itself. Of course, no one can live without passion, and so courtly love evolved as a way for lovers to get their fix of romance, even while they were tied into potentially unsatisfying marriage bonds.

Courtly love was all about the pedestal, and nothing about the practicalities of life. It was never consummated. If a lady requited a knight's love – and the ball was always in her court in that regard – the lovers would simply spend hours gazing at one another, delighting in their secret affair and its covert pleasures.

Traditionally, courtly love occurred between a lovesick knight and an unobtainable lady. To attempt to win his fair maiden's heart, the knight would embark on all sorts of quests and brave deeds. Famous examples of courtly love in literature include the legends of King Arthur's Knights and Petrarch's *Canzoniere* (a sonnet sequence in praise of a woman named Laura); indeed, there's also a parody of the art in Chaucer's bawdy poem *The Miller's Tale*.

The Art of Courtly Love

There was etiquette to abide by when expressing courtly love, based on chivalry and virtue. Manuals explained the strict rules and codes of conduct, and were published as late as the Renaissance.

One of the most famous books, which endures to this day, is Andreas Capellanus's *The Art of Courtly Love*. It is said to reveal life at the court of Eleanor of Aquitaine at Poitiers from 1170 to 1174. Here are some of its guidelines:

✳ 'Every lover regularly turns pale in the presence of his beloved.'

✳ 'When a lover suddenly catches sight of his beloved, his heart palpitates.'

✳ 'He whom the thought of love vexes eats and sleeps very little.'

✳ 'Every act of a lover ends in the thought of his beloved.'

✳ 'A true lover is constantly and without intermission possessed by the thought of his beloved.'

Sound at all familiar?

'The love that lasts the longest is
the love that is never returned.'
W. SOMERSET MAUGHAM

Write Your Own Love Poem

A N original verse – written specially for and dedicated to your lover – will be warmly received on any occasion, be it in honor of your first child's birth, Valentine's Day, moving in together, or the fact that it's Thursday and you're having dinner with each other that night.

If you don't think you're particularly poetic, don't worry – here are some tips to turn all lovers into passionate poets.

* If you're finding it hard to get started, you could try writing an acrostic poem – where the first letter of each line spells out another word. You could use 'Valentine' for Valentine's Day, your lover's name, a place that's special to you both, or more generic words such as 'love', 'heart', 'soulmate' and so on. For example:

    Little did I know when we first met, that you were my
    One. The one above all others. You are more
    Valuable to me than all the riches in the world, more
    Essential to my living than food.

* Think about what you want to say. A technique used

by many writers before they begin a new piece is
something called stream-of-consciousness writing.

Take a blank piece of paper, a pen and a stopwatch.
Spend a minute thinking about your lover, what they
mean to you and what you want to convey to them in
your poem.

Next, note down whatever comes into your head
for a full minute, without trying to make it a poem or
any sort of coherent message. The important thing is
not to worry about what you're writing down, just to
get the words out – even if that means a full page of
'I don't know what to write, I don't know what to
write, I don't know what to write.'

When the minute is up, read what you've written –
perhaps there are some phrases you can use in your
poem, or a starting point from which you can work,
or maybe it will just have focused your mind on the
task ahead.

Repeat this process as necessary.

✳ Remember that poems don't have to rhyme. What is
known as free verse is just as heartfelt as poems that
rhyme, and this tip might save you unnecessary trouble
when you've already linked 'love' with 'dove' and 'above',
and are stuck for another rhyming word that isn't 'shove'.

With free verse, the line breaks come when they feel
natural, and that decision is entirely down to you, the
poet. They might come at the end of a discussion of a
certain topic, after an image has been described, or

♥♥♥

simply when you need to breathe as you're reading the poem aloud.

✳ If you do choose to write a rhyming love poem, you can have fun playing around with the rhyming structure.

Rhyming patterns in literature are described using the letters of the alphabet, which show when rhymes are the same and when they are different. A simple rhyming love poem might use the pattern AABB:

> When first I saw your face,
> I gave immediate chase.
> You've brightened up my life –
> Now, will you be my wife?

You can mix and match different rhyming patterns to your heart's content. Why not try ABAB, ABBA, or the traditional limerick style AABBA? You can also create your own patterns.

✳ Love poems are enlivened by simile and metaphor – saying that a thing is 'like' something else using poetic description; 'your eyes are like the sparkling sea,' for instance, rather than 'your eyes look a bit like the pond on the village green.'

Feel free to draw comparisons between unusual items – it will make your poem that much more original.

✳ Poems are often about feelings, not necessarily facts. A poem that lists everything you and your partner have ever done together has its place, but traditionally your

♥♥♥

poem might describe and appeal to the senses, i.e. your emotions, but also drawing on the sights, sounds, smells, textures and tastes of your love.

✽ Perhaps the most important thing about penning your own love poem is to make it personal, otherwise you might as well have used somebody else's words. Don't be afraid to make reference to specific events, or to use your lover's name.

Ta Da!

When it comes to giving a love poem, presentation is key. There are lots of different ways in which you could give your finished poem to your lover. Here are just a few:

✽ read or sing it aloud (live)

✽ record it on a CD

✽ present your lover with a handwritten, decorated creation featuring the poem (craft shops and haberdashery departments have lots of gorgeous items to enrich your calligraphy – ribbons, glitter, patterns, stickers, and so on)

✽ stitch it on a sampler

✽ ice it on a cake (one for haiku poems)

✽ print it in a national newspaper

Whichever method you choose, your lover is likely to be thrilled by your creative endeavors.

Top Ten Love Poets

If you still need a helping hand, here's a list of ten world-renowned romantic poets, whose collections of love poetry might provide inspiration.

1. Elizabeth Barrett Browning
2. Robert Burns
3. e. e. cummings
4. John Donne
5. Kahlil Gibran
6. John Keats
7. Christina Rossetti
8. Anne Sexton
9. William Shakespeare
10. Alfred, Lord Tennyson

'Love's the only thing I've thought of or read about since I was knee-high. That's what I always dreamed of, of meeting somebody and falling in love. And when that remarkable thing happened, I was going to recite poetry to her for hours about how her heart's an angel's wing and her hair the strings of a heavenly harp. Instead, I got drunk and hollered at her and called her a harpy.'

BEN HECHT

The Secrets of Success

So, is there a secret to long-term happiness with your lover? Romantic novels and films are imbued with the notion of finding The One, your true soulmate from whom you shall never be parted. But, just in case simply being with the right person isn't quite enough to guarantee your eternal happiness together, it doesn't hurt to glean some pearls of wisdom from the experts.

Here, contented couples share their secrets for a lifetime of romantic bliss.

Constance and **Walter Clasper** were officially named Britain's Happiest Couple in February 2002, winning the romantic title in honour of National Marriage Week. Eighty-two-year-old Constance advised: 'Talking and communication are the key.'

It's certainly something they implemented in their own lives. The couple wed in 1937, two years before war broke out in Europe, and five years before Walter was taken prisoner in North Africa. During his incarceration, they sent photographs and love letters to one another across the seas.

Mr. Clasper admitted, 'We love each other today as much as we did when we first met. I tell her I love her every day.'

♥ ♥

Victoria and **Charles Button** were childhood sweethearts, and had a love that remained true long after they married in the 1900s. The year they reached their seventy-seventh wedding anniversary, the couple from South Woodham Ferrers in England both turned 100, and their daughter celebrated her fiftieth wedding anniversary.

Mrs. Button offered her thoughts on the secrets of their remarkable longevity: 'I believe in give and take. You need give to get along and a bit of take as well.'

'He loves me more every day . . . If all married people lived as happily as we do, how many good jokes it would spoil!'
ELIZABETH BARRETT BROWNING,
in a letter to her sisters

In 2005, **Percy** and **Florence Arrowsmith** celebrated the landmark of their eightieth wedding anniversary. Percy explained that their recipe for success was just two words: 'Yes, dear.'

Perhaps unsurprisingly, Mrs. Arrowsmith said they were still very happy.

♥ ♥

♥♥♥♥♥♥♥♥♥♥♥♥♥♥♥♥♥♥♥♥♥♥♥♥♥♥♥♥♥♥♥♥♥♥♥♥♥♥

Anne and **Bert Ivison** from Liverpool first started courting when they were fourteen, having lived on the same street since they were nippers. In 2003, they celebrated their seventy-ninth wedding anniversary – with Anne still sporting the gold bracelet Bert had given her as a teenager.

On the special occasion, Anne had some level-headed words of wisdom, gleaned from her many years of married life: 'My advice is not to let one person be the boss in the relationship. You should both be level.'

> 'Love does not consist in gazing at each other, but in looking together in the same direction.'
> **ANTOINE DE SAINT-EXUPÉRY**

George and **Violet Taylor** received a congratulatory telegram from the Queen of England on the occasion of their platinum wedding anniversary. The happy couple grew up together, living just 50 yards apart as children, and attended the same school before they wed in Chatham in 1933.

Ninety-three-year-old Violet explained: 'We have had arguments, but we never had a really serious quarrel.'

George, ninety-four, further theorized: 'A lot of it is giving way to each other. If one is wrong, the other one accepts it.'

> 'He is not a lover who does not love forever.'
> **EURIPIDES**

♥♥♥♥♥♥♥♥♥♥♥♥♥♥♥♥♥♥♥♥♥♥♥♥♥♥♥♥♥♥♥♥♥♥♥♥♥♥

LONG-DISTANCE LOVE

Eighty-six-year-old Maldwyn Hughes from Bangor, Wales, has an unorthodox recipe for wedded bliss: he lives 3,000 miles away from his wife. Proving the old adage that absence makes the heart grow fonder, he and his wife, seventy-nine-year-old Shirley Luck-Hughes, spend only a few months of the year together – the rest of the time she resides in her native New York State.

'We e-mail each other often,' said Shirley, 'and speak to each other twice a week and send things to each other.'

Maldwyn added, 'I wanted to get married to Shirley, and I have no regrets.'

Fred and **Olive Hodges** wed in 1925. On the occasion of their seventy-seventh wedding anniversary – celebrated in 2002 when they were both aged 102 – Olive revealed her thoughts on what makes a successful relationship: 'It is all about love, give and take and considering the other person. Love is the main thing.'

Every Day, I Love You More

THE big romantic gestures are undeniably great. What's not to love, whether you're making or receiving them? Yet the everyday acts are just as important, if not more so, than those special events organized well in advance.

Here are some suggestions of how to keep the home fires burning day by day, in between the dramatic firework displays.

Wakey, Wakey

Always make time for a morning cuddle just before the alarm starts blaring. Even if it's only for a couple of minutes, you'll start the day in each other's arms, which is a blessing well worth counting.

'Love doesn't make the world go round,
love is what makes the ride worthwhile.'

FRANKLIN JONES

♥♥♥♥♥♥♥♥♥♥♥♥♥♥♥♥♥♥♥♥♥♥♥♥♥♥♥♥♥♥♥♥♥♥♥♥♥♥

I Just Called . . .

At some point during the day – or at many points, depending on your workload – send your lover a text message or e-mail to let them know how much you love them and that you're thinking of them. If they're snowed under, they'll appreciate your thoughtfulness even more.

'If we discovered that we had only five minutes left to say all that we wanted to say, every telephone booth would be occupied by people calling other people to stammer that they loved them.'

CHRISTOPHER MORLEY

Lunchtime Lovin'

Best of all, meet each other for lunch during a hectic working day. The second-best alternative is to make your lover a packed lunch. Sporadically include special treats like a piece of mozzarella in their chicken-slice sandwiches, a tasty dressing on their salad, or a packet of chocolate buttons for dessert.

TIP!

Why not save your partner's picture as the screensaver or desktop wallpaper on your office computer? You might not be together physically, but this way you'll still get to see their gorgeous smile time and again.

♥♥♥♥♥♥♥♥♥♥♥♥♥♥♥♥♥♥♥♥♥♥♥♥♥♥♥♥♥♥♥♥♥♥♥♥♥♥

Express Delivery

Brighten up your partner's day at the office with an unexpected delivery of flowers, wine or other gifts such as music or books.

'Love is friendship set on fire.'
JEREMY TAYLOR

Hi Honey, I'm Home!

Never stint on that greeting kiss. No matter where you're rushing off to later that evening, or how many kids you've got to feed and bathe in the next hour, take a luxurious moment to embrace your lover and give them a lingering kiss.

'Love is the master key that opens the gates of happiness.'
OLIVER WENDELL HOLMES

Heavenly Housework

If you undertake housework together, it ceases to be a chore. Put some favorite music on the stereo, and dance around and sing in the kitchen in a fabulous musical number until the washing-up's all done. Though it can be fun to play house together, your lover will always appreciate it if you offer to clean up solo, especially if they're dead on their feet.

♥♥♥♥♥♥♥♥♥♥♥♥♥♥♥♥♥♥♥♥♥♥♥♥♥♥♥♥♥♥♥♥♥♥♥♥♥

Smile, Smile, Smile

Give your partner at least one truly heartfelt smile every day. Let it stretch across your face and reach the furthest corners of your eyes while looking deep in your lover's eyes.

> 'I smile whenever I see him. He always knows how thrilled I am that he's there with me.'
> **MELANIE GRIFFITH**,
> married to actor Antonio Banderas

Cozy Comfort

Prepare thoughtful things to make your lover's life more comfortable. For example, place their towel on a heated rail or radiator while they shower, so they can wrap themselves in warm cotton as soon as they step out.

Light a fire in the winter, buy your partner thick woollen socks to keep cold feet warm, and don't forget the furry hot-water bottle in between the sheets as the nights draw in.

> 'We are each of us angels with only one wing.
> And we can only fly embracing each other.'
> **LUCIANO DE CRESCENZO**

♥♥♥♥♥♥♥♥♥♥♥♥♥♥♥♥♥♥♥♥♥♥♥♥♥♥♥♥♥♥♥♥♥♥♥♥♥

Listen to My Heart

Take the time to talk. Be it over dinner, in bed or over the phone, have a real conversation with your partner every day. Don't just exchange small talk or have two concurrent monologues.

Listen to each other. Find out what you've each been up to: the daily hopes and fears, the stresses and successes that make up living life. Help and support each other every day: with words, with actions – and also with massages when times are tough.

'There is no remedy for love
but to love more.'
HENRY DAVID THOREAU

Sleep Tight

Never forget to say good night, and never let the sun set on an argument. At bedtime, snuggle up close together and hold each other tight all night.

'So, fall asleep love, loved by me . . . for I know love,
I am loved by thee.'
ROBERT BROWNING